S0-AEJ-947

Gospel Connections for Teens

This book helped me connect the Gospel to my everyday life. It helped me recognize my own personal connection to the Gospel message and it helped me identify others who inspire me by their example.

—Brigette Brennan, a teen editor

Gospel Connections for Teens is a book for any teen who is looking for more out of the Sunday readings. It is matter-of-fact, speaks to teens on their level, and challenges teens to think about their lives. I was especially pleased to see the questions at the start of each reflection, challenging the reader to apply the Sunday readings to their daily lives. Any time we can help young people get more out of the Eucharist, our "source and summit," we should take full advantage of it.

—Matthew Miller, director, Youth Liturgical Leadership Program, Saint Meinrad School of Theology, Saint Meinrad, Indiana

How exciting it is to find a book that brings the Scriptures, real-life experiences, and questions for reflection together in an easy-to-use format. Brost suggests that readers "take 5" to examine, "take 5" to read, and "take 10" to reflect. I suggest we each take all the time necessary to use this book in our ministry with young people—and even for our own spiritual journey.

—Michael Norman, associate director, Office of Religious Education, Archdiocese of Los Angeles

Through this book I am able to relate my experiences to the Gospels and Jesus' life on earth.

—Celine, a teen editor

What struck me most about this book is how it immediately connects the Gospel readings to our everyday lives. This is a challenge, to see Jesus Christ in the ordinary and in our everyday experiences. There is also a gentle challenge to live out the words we hear proclaimed each week at the Eucharist. Corey has a great way of showing us that living a life as a person of faith requires action, and this faith-filled life is so needed in today's world.

What I liked most about the book were the reflections on Holy Week. The powerful words and images took me on my own personal retreat. I believe teens will be enriched as they turn each page and encounter Jesus and his followers in their lives. They will realize they are not alone on this faith journey—and that one of their companions can be the Scriptures.

—Anna Scally, president, Cornerstone Media Inc.

Gospel Connections for Teens

Reflections for Sunday Mass, Cycle B

Corey Brost, CSV

Saint Mary's Press®

Genuine recycled paper with 10% post-consumer waste.
5094300

Scripture texts used in this work are taken from the *Lectionary for Mass for Use in the Dioceses of the United States of America,* second typical edition, volume 1. Copyright © 1970, 1997, 1998 by the Confraternity of Christian Doctrine, Inc., Washington, D.C. All rights reserved. No part of this work may be reproduced or transmitted in any form or by any means, electronic or mechanical, including photocopying, recording, or by any information storage and retrieval system, without permission in writing from the copyright owner.

The publishing team included Brian Singer-Towns, development editor; Lorraine Kilmartin, reviewer; prepress and manufacturing coordinated by the prepublication and production services departments of Saint Mary's Press.

Copyright © 2005 by Saint Mary's Press, Christian Brothers Publications, 702 Terrace Heights, Winona, MN 55987-1318, www.smp.org. All rights reserved. No part of this book may be reproduced by any means without the written permission of the publisher.

Printed in the United States of America

Printing: 9 8 7 6 5 4 3 2

Year: 2013 12 11 10 09 08 07 06 05

ISBN-13: 978-0-88489-848-1
ISBN-10: 0-88489-848-2

Library of Congress Cataloging-in-Publication Data
Brost, Corey.
Gospel connections for teens : reflections for Sunday mass / Corey Brost.
    p. cm.
ISBN 0-88489-848-2 (pbk.)
    1. Bible. N.T. Gospels—Meditations—Juvenile literature. 2. Church year meditations—Juvenile literature. I. Title.
BS2555.54.B76 2005
242'.63—dc22
                                                              2005000795

I dedicate this book to my mom, Mary Claire Brost. Mom, I never would have known God without your strength, courage, and faith. I owe my faith—and any good it has done me or others—to you.

This book was a joint effort. Four teens worked diligently as an editing team to help me refine each reflection. Their input was invaluable. So, thanks to Brigette Brennan, Mark Chaput, John Leahy, and Celine Fitzgerald. Your willingness to grow closer to Christ has inspired me.

Contents

Introduction

I wrote this book because I never had one like it when I was a teen. I struggled each Sunday to connect the Gospel to my teen joys and struggles. I hope this book helps you do just that.

First, a brief explanation. In the Church liturgical year, the Sunday Gospel readings follow a three-year cycle. This book covers the second year of that cycle, called cycle B. In cycle B most of the Gospel readings are taken from the Gospel of Mark.

Here's how you use this book, then. Look at the chart that follows this introduction. Look up the date of the coming Sunday in the chart, and you will find the correct reflection. Commit to spending twenty minutes each week to reflect on the Gospel before you go to Mass. Use the book's reflection process or create your own. Then go to Mass on Sunday and compare your reflection to the homily. You might even want to get a few friends together over coffee or snacks during the week to compare thoughts on the readings.

Because of space limitations, I've edited a few lines out of some of the Gospel passages. The Scripture citations at the top of the page indicate the complete Gospel passage for that Sunday. If I've shortened the passage, you will see a second citation immediately following the passage indicating the exact verses I used.

All but a few of the names in the reflections are made up, though all the people I mention are real people I've come across in life and ministry. May the time you spend reflecting on God's holy word be blessed.

Reflection Chart

Sunday Gospel Reflection	Page No.	2005–2006	2008–2009	2011–2012
1st Sunday of Advent	14	Nov. 27	Nov. 30	Nov. 27
2nd Sunday of Advent	16	Dec. 4	Dec. 7	Dec. 4
3rd Sunday of Advent	18	Dec. 11	Dec. 14	Dec. 11
4th Sunday of Advent	20	Dec. 18	Dec. 21	Dec. 18
Christmas (Midnight Mass)	22	Dec. 25	Dec. 25	Dec. 25
Feast of the Holy Family	24	Dec. 30	Dec. 28	Dec. 30
Mary, Mother of God	26	Jan. 1	Jan. 1	Jan. 1
Feast of the Epiphany	28	Jan. 8	Jan. 4	Jan. 8
Baptism of the Lord	30	Jan. 9	Jan. 11	Jan. 9
2nd Sunday of Ordinary Time	32	Jan. 15	Jan. 18	Jan. 15
3rd Sunday of Ordinary Time	34	Jan. 22	Jan. 25	Jan. 22
4th Sunday of Ordinary Time	36	Jan. 29	Feb. 1	Jan. 29
5th Sunday of Ordinary Time	38	Feb. 5	Feb. 8	Feb. 5
6th Sunday of Ordinary Time	40	Feb. 12	Feb. 15	Feb. 12
7th Sunday of Ordinary Time	42	Feb. 19	Feb. 22	Feb. 19
8th Sunday of Ordinary Time	44	Feb. 26		
1st Sunday of Lent	46	Mar. 5	Mar. 1	Feb. 26
2nd Sunday of Lent	48	Mar. 12	Mar. 8	Mar. 4
3rd Sunday of Lent	50	Mar. 19	Mar. 15	Mar. 11
4th Sunday of Lent	52	Mar. 26	Mar. 22	Mar. 18
5th Sunday of Lent	54	April 2	Mar. 29	Mar. 25
Palm Sunday (The Passion)	56	April 9	April 5	April 1
Easter Sunday	58	April 16	April 12	April 8
2nd Sunday of Easter	60	April 23	April 19	April 15
3rd Sunday of Easter	62	April 30	April 26	April 22
4th Sunday of Easter	64	May 7	May 3	April 29
5th Sunday of Easter	66	May 14	May 10	May 6
6th Sunday of Easter	68	May 21	May 17	May 13
7th Sunday of Easter	70	May 28	May 24	May 20

Reflections on the Sunday Gospel Readings

Wake Up! Jesus Is Here Right Now

Take :05 Examine

How did I live out last week's Gospel message? What was tough? What was rewarding?

Take :05 Read

Jesus said to his disciples: "Be watchful! Be alert! You do not know when the time will come. It is like a man traveling abroad. He leaves home and places his servants in charge, each with his own work, and orders the gatekeeper to be on the watch. Watch, therefore; you do not know when the Lord of the house is coming, whether in the evening, or at midnight, or at cockcrow, or in the morning. May he not come suddenly and find you sleeping. What I say to you, I say to all: 'Watch!'"

Stop and think. Do you ever feel alone when you need help with a problem? Do you ever doubt whether your life really makes a difference? A lot of teens often feel isolated or unimportant.

If you have ever had those feelings, pay attention to Jesus' words: "Be alert! Watch!" Jesus wants you to know that God's help is staring you right in the face. His mission for you is right in front of you.

During Advent we join with Catholics around the world to remember that God sent Jesus once and will send him again at the world's end. Why? Because we need him. We need his help because life is just too hard sometimes. We need his vision because we sometimes miss the work he wants us to do in this messed-up world.

Unfortunately life gets so busy that we often miss the many ways Christ tries to comfort us or send us to others. Advent is a great time to slow down and be watchful. When you hurt, be alert; Christ is sending people to help you. Pray for help to see them and the humility to accept their help. When others hurt, Christ wants to send you. Like the servants in the reading, Christ has important work for you to do in healing this broken world. Pray for help to see those people whose lives you can change.

Take these four weeks of Advent to pray more often. Actively look for how much Christ loves you and needs you. Let Advent remind you that Jesus really comes into the world *every day*. But we miss that unless we watch for Christ, accept Christ's love, and help others in Christ's name.

Take :10 Reflect

If a word or phrase from the Gospel grabs your heart, sit quietly for several minutes and repeat it to yourself, asking God to show you how it applies to your life. Or, reflect and possibly journal on the following question:

- When I look at the people in my daily life, who are the ones Christ is sending to help me, and who are the ones Christ is showing me I could help?

Do You Know John the Baptist?

Take :05 Examine

How did I live out last week's Gospel message? What was tough? What was rewarding?

Take :05 Read

The beginning of the gospel of Jesus Christ the Son of God.
As it is written in Isaiah the prophet:
Behold, I am sending my messenger ahead of you;
he will prepare your way.
A voice of one crying out in the desert:
"Prepare the way of the Lord,
make straight his paths."
John the Baptist appeared in the desert proclaiming a baptism of repentance for the forgiveness of sins. People of the whole Judean countryside and all the inhabitants of Jerusalem were going out to him and were being baptized by him in the Jordan River as they acknowledged their sins. John was clothed in camel's hair, with a leather belt around his waist. He fed on locusts and wild honey. And this is what he proclaimed: "One mightier than I is coming after me. I am not worthy to stoop and loosen the thongs of his sandals. I have baptized you with water; he will baptize you with the Holy Spirit."

John the Baptist. Who was this guy?

Do you know someone who stands up for people who are being put down? How about someone who tells friends it's crazy to use alcohol or drugs? What about someone who takes a stand on political issues, arguing for peace or pro-life values? Do you know a person who won't laugh at racist jokes?

If you know any of those people, you know John the Baptist. He had the guts to publicly challenge people to follow God's way—a path of compassion, forgiveness, repentance, and sacrifice for poor people. He called on ordinary people and the rulers of his day to change their lives. He pointed to Jesus as the example to follow. In the end his courage cost him his life when King Herod imprisoned and murdered him.

It's tough speaking the truth. I know teens who are mocked by their peers because they publicly demonstrated against war. But they did it anyway because they read the Gospel and they saw protesting for peace as Jesus' way. They had guts. Look around. Other people in our world, probably at your school, are showing similar courage. People like Bono, who speaks out for AIDS victims in Africa. Doesn't our broken world need more people who are willing to stand for God, even when it costs them?

Who was John the Baptist? Why not let it be *you* this Advent.

Take :10 Reflect

If a word or phrase from the Gospel grabs your heart, sit quietly for several minutes, repeating it to yourself and asking God to show you how it applies to your life. Or, reflect and possibly journal on the following question:

- How can I be more like John the Baptist at school, at home, or at work?

It Costs to Be "The Baptist"

Take :05 Examine

How did I live out last week's Gospel message? What was tough? What was rewarding?

Take :05 Read

A man named John was sent from God. He came for testimony, to testify to the light, so that all might believe through him. He was not the light, but came to testify to the light.

And this is the testimony of John. When the Jews from Jerusalem sent priests and Levites to him to ask him, "Who are you?" he admitted and did not deny it, but admitted, "I am not the Christ."

So they asked him, "What are you then? Are you Elijah?" And he said, "I am not." "Are you the Prophet?" He answered, "No." So they said to him, "Who are you, so we can give an answer to those who sent us? What do you have to say for yourself?" He said:

"I am the voice of one crying out in the desert,
'make straight the way of the Lord,'"

as Isaiah the prophet said. Some Pharisees were also sent. They asked him, "Why then do you baptize if you are not the Christ or Elijah or the Prophet?" John answered them, "I baptize with water; but there is one among you whom you do not recognize, the one who is coming after me, whose sandal strap I am not worthy to untie." This happened in Bethany across the Jordan, where John was baptizing.

"Back off! Who do you think you are?"

So many times as a teen I kept quiet when I needed to speak up. Or I lashed out and attacked people who disagreed with me. Scientists talk about this as the flight-or-fight response, two reactions that seem built into us for responding to an attack.

When you stand up for what is right, some people will try to quiet you with hostile looks or comments. That's what happened to John the Baptist. The people asking questions in this Gospel came from the religious leaders who eventually helped kill Jesus. They came because John's message, like Jesus' message, threatened them and they wanted him to back off. His words called them to change, to give up their status, power, and privilege. John didn't back off. But he also didn't attack them. John found a third way that went beyond flight or fight.

This Advent, if you choose to be John the Baptist, you'll face the same thing. There's no way around it. Standing up for what's right, for the weak and vulnerable, almost always angers some people. How will you handle it? Will you follow John's example and stand strong for your Christian beliefs without retaliating?

Sometimes you'll fall short. If so, don't get down on yourself. Pray for strength to stay firm but peaceful next time. Find the people in your life—peers and adults—who will back you. God gave them to you for support in tough situations.

Through it all, remember that God believes in you and that you make a difference each time you try to take that tough stand.

Take :10 Reflect

If a word or phrase from the Gospel grabs your heart, sit quietly for several minutes, repeating it to yourself and asking God to show you how it applies to your life. Or, reflect and possibly journal on the following question:

- Who can I turn to for support when I'm attacked for living like John the Baptist?

God Just Makes No Sense

Take :05 Examine

How did I live out last week's Gospel message? What was tough? What was rewarding?

Take :05 Read

The angel Gabriel was sent from God to a town of Galilee called Nazareth, to a virgin betrothed to a man named Joseph, of the house of David, and the virgin's name was Mary. And coming to her, he said, "Hail, full of grace! The Lord is with you." But she was greatly troubled at what was said and pondered what sort of greeting this might be. Then the angel said to her, "Do not be afraid, Mary, for you have found favor with God.

"Behold, you will conceive in your womb and bear a son, and you shall name him Jesus. He will be great and will be called Son of the Most High, and the Lord God will give him the throne of David his father, and he will rule over the house of Jacob forever, and of his kingdom there will be no end." But Mary said to the angel, "How can this be, since I have no relations with a man?" And the angel said to her in reply, "The Holy Spirit will come upon you, and the power of the Most High will overshadow you. Therefore the child to be born will be called holy, the Son of God. . . . Mary said, "Behold, I am the handmaid of the Lord. May it be done to me according to your word." Then the angel departed from her. (Luke 1:26–35,38)

Many students thought they were crazy. Eight high school seniors decided to help start a retreat program at their school. And they heard it all: "Who would want to do that?" "Are you a Jesus freak now?" "What a waste of time."

It made no sense—unless you know God.

Go back two thousand years. A teen girl hears God's call. She lives in a culture where young women are viewed as men's property. She lives in a region, Galilee, looked down on by the rest of Israel. Yet God chose her to change the world by bearing Jesus.

It made no sense—unless you know God.

Mary must have known her Jewish scripture. She must have grown up learning that she could trust God's love, trust it enough to risk her life by agreeing to bear Jesus as an unwed mother. *You* can trust this God as well. You might think you can't make a difference. Trust God and risk a try. You might feel unlovable at times. Trust God and reach out for the friends God *will* put in your life. You might think you can't take tough stands for what's right. Trust God and feel holy strength fill your soul.

Oh, and what about those crazy high school seniors? They started their retreat program. It ran for nine years and helped more than five hundred teens, changing some of their lives dramatically.

It made no sense to many—unless they knew God.

Take :10 Reflect

If a word or phrase from the Gospel grabs your heart, sit quietly for several minutes, repeating it to yourself and asking God to show you how it applies to your life. Or, reflect and possibly journal on the following question:

- This week how can I take a risk for God that makes sense only to those who know God?

Jesus: Born for Life's Mess

Take :05 Examine

How did I live out last week's Gospel message? What was
tough? What was rewarding?

Take :05 Read

*And Joseph too went up from Galilee from the town of Nazareth
to Judea, to the city of David that is called Bethlehem, because
he was of the house and family of David, to be enrolled with
Mary, his betrothed, who was with child. While they were there,
the time came for her to have her child, and she gave birth to
her firstborn son. She wrapped him in swaddling clothes and laid
him in a manger, because there was no room for them in the
inn.*

*Now there were shepherds in that region living in the fields
and keeping the night watch over their flock. The angel of the
Lord appeared to them and the glory of the Lord shone around
them, and they were struck with great fear. The angel said to
them, "Do not be afraid; for behold, I proclaim to you good news
of great joy that will be for all the people. For today in the city of
David a savior has been born for you who is Christ and Lord.
And this will be a sign for you: you will find an infant wrapped in
swaddling clothes and lying in a manger." And suddenly there
was a multitude of the heavenly host with the angel, praising
God and saying:*

"Glory to God in the highest
and on earth peace to those on whom his favor rests."

(Luke 2:4–14)

Our Christmas traditions are a bit off.

Today, we clean up the house. We hang greenery. We light up our living room with a tree. We put out pleasant-smelling candles. We entertain well-dressed friends and neighbors who drop by for a visit.

The first Christmas was pretty different. Jesus was born in an open animal pen. All in all, the scene of Jesus' birth was a smelly mess. No one would buy a candle scented like Jesus' first home. As for the visitors, many Jews saw shepherds as the dregs of society. And that is what's great about Christmas! God became flesh to enter our mess.

God's not afraid of messes. God seeks them out to transform them. You might live in a well-decorated home this Christmas. But we've all got a mess somewhere. You might be fighting with someone. You might feel friendless. Your grades might be low. Your self-confidence might be nil. Where do you need God's peace this Christmas?

Certainly our world has plenty of messes also. Violence, loneliness, and poverty cry out for people like you to bring tidings of good news as volunteers. Friends, family, or classmates might need your help with a problem. You can be God's peace this Christmas.

So dive into life's mess this Christmas. You'll find our Savior.

Take :10 Reflect

If a word or phrase from the Gospel grabs your heart, sit quietly for several minutes, repeating it to yourself and asking God to show you how it applies to your life. Or, reflect and possibly journal on the following question:

- What is the greatest gift God has given me or could give me this Christmas to help me be a person of peace?

Catching the Faith at Home

Take :05 Examine

How did I live out last week's Gospel message? What was tough? What was rewarding?

Take :05 Read

Now there was a man in Jerusalem whose name was Simeon. This man was righteous and devout, awaiting the consolation of Israel, and the Holy Spirit was upon him. It had been revealed to him by the Holy Spirit that he should not see death before he had seen the Christ of the Lord. He came in the Spirit into the temple; and when the parents brought in the child Jesus to perform the custom of the law in regard to him, he took him into his arms and blessed God, saying:

"Now, Master, you may let your servant go
in peace, according to your word,
for my eyes have seen your salvation,
which you prepared in sight of all the peoples,
a light for revelation to the Gentiles,
and glory for your people Israel."

The child's father and mother were amazed at what was said about him. . . . There was also a prophetess, Anna, the daughter of Phanuel, of the tribe of Asher. She was advanced in years, having lived seven years with her husband after her marriage, and then as a widow until she was eighty-four. She never left the temple, but worshiped night and day with fasting and prayer. And coming forward at that very time, she gave thanks to God and spoke about the child to all who were awaiting the redemption of Jerusalem. (Luke 2:25–28,36–38)

It's my mom's voice I hear.

During those tough times when I'm hoping God will help me out—it's her voice that echoes, "God will get me through this." My family had some tough times when I was a kid. But my mom always hung tougher. Her faith in God kept her—and us—going. Her faith sparked mine. It left seeds that helped me grow into an adult disciple.

I'm convinced the same was true for Jesus. This week we see his parents, faithful Jews, bring him to the Temple. How many times in his life did he hear them say, "God will get us through this"? Jesus, fully human, couldn't have become the radical witness for God without his faithful parents.

Have you ever asked a parent or other family member about faith? Why not do that this week? Ask a parent, a grandparent, or another family member about his or her relationship with God. Ask what he or she thinks a Christian's mission in the world should be. Listen for his or her questions and hopes. Look for tips on finding God in tough times.

Remember, faith is somewhat like the flu: if we want to catch it, we need to hang out with people who've been infected for a while and listen to their stories.

Take :10 Reflect

If a word or phrase from the Gospel grabs your heart, sit quietly for several minutes, repeating it to yourself and asking God to show you how it applies to your life. Or, reflect and possibly journal on the following question:

- Which family member or older person of faith can I ask this week about her or his relationship with God?

Resolve to Pray Like Mary

Take :05 Examine

How did I live out last week's Gospel message? What was tough? What was rewarding?

Take :05 Read

The shepherds went in haste to Bethlehem and found Mary and Joseph, and the infant lying in the manger. When they saw this, they made known the message that had been told them about this child. All who heard it were amazed by what had been told them by the shepherds. And Mary kept all these things, reflecting on them in her heart. Then the shepherds returned, glorifying and praising God for all they had heard and seen, just as it had been told to them.

When eight days were completed for his circumcision, he was named Jesus, the name given him by the angel before he was conceived in the womb.

I recently met Brian while serving at a soup kitchen. He was about nineteen and looking for direction in life. To find it, he had decided to volunteer for a year at the soup kitchen, where he lived in a dorm with other young adults who prepare the nightly meals.

The key to finding direction, he said, would be his service and a lot of prayer. Reflection on his volunteering would help him find a meaningful future.

Brian's doing just what Mary did two thousand years ago. Mary didn't receive a fax or an e-mail from God laying out her role in Jesus' life. She had to learn God's will just like we do—by watching the world and praying about her part in it. That's what the Gospel means when it says that she "kept all these things, reflecting on them in her heart."

Luke shows us Mary, the prayerful woman, who watched the circumstances around Jesus' birth closely and then asked God to provide direction for her future. I believe Mary became Jesus' first disciple—and our model for discipleship—only because she lived a disciplined prayer life.

And that's true for us. We can't be true disciples without following her example. Don't disconnect prayer from your life experiences. In fact, you'll only sense God in your life by prayerfully reviewing your life daily. Ask daily questions in prayer like: Who showed me God's love today? Who challenged me to be more Christian today? Did my life further or block the Gospel today? What does all this mean for my actions tomorrow and into the future?

The more you ask those questions in prayer and share your insights with other Christians, the more you'll see God's activity in your life. And the more you'll want God's future guidance—just like Mary and Brian.

Sound like a good New Year's resolution?

Take :10 Reflect

If a word or phrase from the Gospel grabs your heart, sit quietly for several minutes, repeating it to yourself and asking God to show you how it applies to your life. Or, reflect and possibly journal on one of the following questions:

- How do I pray over my daily experiences? What could I do to strengthen my prayer life this new year?

Which Star Do You Follow?

Take :05 Examine

How did I live out last week's Gospel message? What was tough? What was rewarding?

Take :05 Read

When Jesus was born in Bethlehem of Judea, in the days of King Herod, behold, magi from the east arrived in Jerusalem, saying, "Where is the newborn king of the Jews? We saw his star at its rising and have come to do him homage." When King Herod heard this, he was greatly troubled, and all Jerusalem with him. Assembling all the chief priests and the scribes of the people, he inquired of them where the Christ was to be born. They said to him, "In Bethlehem of Judea, for thus it has been written through the prophet:

And you, Bethlehem, land of Judah,
     are by no means least among the rulers of Judah;
since from you shall come a ruler,
     who is to shepherd my people Israel."

Then Herod called the magi secretly and ascertained from them the time of the star's appearance. He sent them to Bethlehem and said, "Go and search diligently for the child. When you have found him, bring me word, that I too may go and do him homage." After their audience with the king they set out. And behold, the star that they had seen at its rising preceded them, until it came and stopped over the place where the child was. They were overjoyed at seeing the star, and on entering the house they saw the child with Mary his mother. They prostrated themselves and did him homage. Then they opened their treasures and offered him gifts of gold, frankincense, and myrrh.

And having been warned in a dream not to return to Herod, they departed for their country by another way.

Many stars shine brightly in our nation: athletes, politicians, musicians, corporate CEOs. And many people—young and old—search for happiness by following them. This week's Gospel focuses on another star and another search. In it the Magi come to Jerusalem following a star they believe will lead them to the newborn "King of the Jews."

Which star are you following? Where is your search leading you?

We live in a world that often glorifies fame over service, money over people, and the national flag over the Christian cross. These are embedded in slogans you hear every day: "Look out for number one," "Get what you can" or "Back your country, right or wrong."

But there is a different path, one that leads to life to the fullest and a better world, a path that ends at that small house in Bethlehem. You will find it through prayer, worship, service, and political action for Christian causes. It's not an easy path, but Christ calls us to walk it. Like the Magi, your faith will end up scaring some powerful people. But God believes in you, has chosen you, and will walk with you through it all.

Take :10 Reflect

If a word or phrase from the Gospel grabs your heart, sit quietly for several minutes, repeating it to yourself and asking God to show you how it applies to your life. Or, reflect and possibly journal on the following question:

- What other "stars" tempt you to follow them?

You Are God's Beloved

Take :05 Examine

How did I live out last week's Gospel message? What was tough? What was rewarding?

Take :05 Read

This is what John the Baptist proclaimed: "One mightier than I is coming after me. I am not worthy to stoop and loosen the thongs of his sandals. I have baptized you with water; he will baptize you with the Holy Spirit."

It happened in those days that Jesus came from Nazareth of Galilee and was baptized in the Jordan by John. On coming up out of the water he saw the heavens being torn open and the Spirit, like a dove, descending upon him. And a voice came from the heavens, "You are my beloved Son; with you I am well pleased."

Sometimes, as a teen, I would get sick of being Catholic. It seemed like nothing more than rules and threats. I've known a lot of teens since then who've felt the same way.

But this Gospel shows us what it's really all about. Catholicism is about God's love for us and how that can change the world.

Notice: at Jesus' Baptism God didn't provide him with a list of "do's and don'ts." God's love descended upon him, and Jesus became aware of how important he was to God. You know what followed. Jesus traveled through the countryside healing the sick, helping the poor, and calling for religious and political reform.

Faith doesn't grow from fear of breaking God's rules. Faith comes from a deepening awareness of how much God loves us. The more aware we are of God's love, the more we naturally avoid sins that hurt us and others, and the rules of Christian life make more sense. It can be tough to remember how lovable we are. It's easy to focus on our failures. It's easy to see only where we don't measure up. It's easy to stay down when other people put us there.

God wants to free you with love. God wants you to see yourself as Christ sees you—full of talent and potential waiting to explode into a wounded world. This week, each morning, stand in front of the mirror for a moment and think only about your talents. Imagine God's voice telling you that *"you* are my beloved; with *you* I'm well pleased." Let that guide your life, and watch how you make a difference for others.

Take :10 Reflect

If a word or phrase from the Gospel grabs your heart, sit quietly for several minutes, repeating it to yourself and asking God to show you how it applies to your life. Or, reflect and possibly journal on the following question:

- Who in my life reminds me of God's love and God's faith in me?

Second Sunday of Ordinary Time
John 1:35–42

Looking in All the Right Places

Take :05 Examine

How did I live out last week's Gospel message? What was tough? What was rewarding?

Take :05 Read

John was standing with two of his disciples, and as he watched Jesus walk by, he said, "Behold, the Lamb of God." The two disciples heard what he said and followed Jesus. Jesus turned and saw them following him and said to them, "What are you looking for?" They said to him, "Rabbi"—which translated means Teacher—, "where are you staying?" He said to them, "Come, and you will see." So they went and saw where he was staying, and they stayed with him that day. It was about four in the afternoon. Andrew, the brother of Simon Peter, was one of the two who heard John and followed Jesus. He first found his own brother Simon and told him, "We have found the Messiah"—which is translated Christ. Then he brought him to Jesus. Jesus looked at him and said, "You are Simon the son of John; you will be called Cephas"—which is translated Peter.

"I struggle with my faith," many teens have told me, "because I just can't find God in this world."

They were searching just like the Apostles in today's Gospel. The Apostles were looking for God and God's hope in a world full of suffering and confusion. That's why they were following John the Baptist. He pointed them to Jesus. After following Jesus to where he was staying, they left excitedly to tell more people about "the Messiah."

Today Jesus is just as real in our world, but many people don't believe in him because they aren't looking in the right places. We only need to spend time where he is "staying" in order to find him. And he stays today right where he stayed when he walked the earth two thousand years ago—with people who suffer and aren't the most popular to be with. Today you will find our Messiah if you spend time in soup kitchens or shelters, in hospitals or nursing homes, at lunch tables with the kids who have few friends. You'll see our Messiah working in the people who help others and the people we often write off.

Go spend time with him where he stays. Watch as your faith comes alive. Then follow him.

Take :10 Reflect

If a word or phrase from the Gospel grabs your heart, sit quietly for several minutes and repeat it to yourself, asking God to show you how it applies to your life. Or, reflect and possibly journal on one of the following questions:

- How much time do I spend just on myself? Do I look for Jesus enough by reaching out to people who suffer?

Just Drop It!

How did I live out last week's Gospel message? What was tough? What was rewarding?

After John had been arrested, Jesus came to Galilee proclaiming the gospel of God: "This is the time of fulfillment. The kingdom of God is at hand. Repent, and believe in the gospel."

As he passed by the Sea of Galilee, he saw Simon and his brother Andrew casting their nets into the sea; they were fishermen. Jesus said to them, "Come after me, and I will make you fishers of men." Then they abandoned their nets and followed him. He walked along a little farther and saw James, the son of Zebedee, and his brother John. They too were in a boat mending their nets. Then he called them. So they left their father Zebedee in the boat along with the hired men and followed him.

Don was a freshman looking for trouble. He partied with seniors. He started fights. He got drunk. Then he went on retreat—and things changed. He heard a voice in his heart calling him to drop his lifestyle and follow a different path.

He followed. As a senior, Don was leading retreats, working with homeless families, and encouraging his friends to stay away from drugs and alcohol. He was changing lives, and he was very happy.

That's what Jesus' call does to people. It changed people two thousand years ago and it changes people today. And the result is always the same—the people who hear his call and follow him end up changing their part of the world.

But they *always* have to drop something, because the call is costly. The Apostles dropped their fishing nets, the only way of life they knew. People today who follow Jesus might talk about dropping things like selfishness, a need for power, dreams of great wealth, or a thirst for revenge.

Everyone has to drop something. Take time in prayer. Jesus will help you figure out what you need to drop. Yes, his call will cost you. But, boy, is it worth the cost!

Take :10 Reflect

If a word or phrase from the Gospel grabs your heart, sit quietly for several minutes and repeat it to yourself, asking God to show you how it applies to your life. Or, reflect and possibly journal on the following question:

- What do I need to drop right now to follow Jesus more closely?

Take On the Demons

Take :05 Examine

How did I live out last week's Gospel message? What was tough? What was rewarding?

Take :05 Read

Then they came to Capernaum, and on the sabbath Jesus entered the synagogue and taught. The people were astonished at his teaching, for he taught them as one having authority and not as the scribes. In their synagogue was a man with an unclean spirit; he cried out, "What have you to do with us, Jesus of Nazareth? Have you come to destroy us? I know who you are—the Holy One of God!" Jesus rebuked him and said, "Quiet! Come out of him!" The unclean spirit convulsed him and with a loud cry came out of him. All were amazed and asked one another, "What is this? A new teaching with authority. He commands even the unclean spirits and they obey him." His fame spread everywhere throughout the whole region of Galilee.

Jesus' word frees people.

Take Mary. She was a high school senior and really into partying. Her friends convinced her to go on a school retreat. Within days after the retreat, she walked into the school's campus ministry office. She told her campus minister that she used drugs daily, before, during, and after school, and needed help. The conversation started her on the road to recovery.

Yes, Jesus' word still frees people.

The Gospel tells about Jesus liberating a man held hostage by a demon. People were amazed. They believed, because Jesus stood against those forces that compete with God for control of people's lives. They saw his words powerfully change people's lives. We might see demons differently in our day and age, but they still hold people hostage. Sex, fear, drugs, alcohol, prejudice, greed, nationalism—it's all too easy for people to lose control to these unholy forces, forces that hurt themselves and others.

Jesus' words offer freedom. And we need more people who are willing to share those words. Live your life standing against all those forces that compete with God for control of your life and the lives of others. Pray for the courage to speak up like Jesus, and challenge people whose lives are held hostage by modern-day demons.

You too will amaze people.

Take :10 Reflect

If a word or phrase from the Gospel grabs your heart, sit quietly for several minutes and repeat it to yourself, asking God to show you how it applies to your life. Or, reflect and possibly journal on the following questions:

- Am I or is someone in my life struggling with a modern-day demon? What can I do about it?

Fifth Sunday of Ordinary Time
Mark 1:29–39

Do You Have the Cure?

Take :05 Examine

How did I live out last week's Gospel message? What was
tough? What was rewarding?

Take :05 Read

*On leaving the synagogue Jesus entered the house of Simon and
Andrew with James and John. Simon's mother-in-law lay sick with
a fever. They immediately told him about her. He approached,
grasped her hand, and helped her up. Then the fever left her and
she waited on them.*

*When it was evening, after sunset, they brought to him all
who were ill or possessed by demons. The whole town was
gathered at the door. He cured many who were sick with various
diseases, and he drove out many demons, not permitting them to
speak because they knew him.*

*Rising very early before dawn, he left and went off to a
deserted place, where he prayed. Simon and those who were
with him pursued him and on finding him said, "Everyone is
looking for you." He told them, "Let us go on to the nearby
villages that I may preach there also. For this purpose have I
come." So he went into their synagogues, preaching and driving
out demons throughout the whole of Galilee.*

Mother Teresa of Calcutta was a healer.

She and her sisters welcomed the abandoned sick and
cared for them until they died. She didn't make their
diseases go away, but she cured some of the worst symptoms—isolation and loneliness. Her patients died with
people who loved and respected them.

Scripture scholars debate over the type of illnesses Jesus healed. They also debate over how he did it. But they agree on one important thing: he cured some of the worst symptoms. In Ancient Israel, people with serious diseases were often kicked out of town because religious laws forbid others from coming too close to them. Or, some people thought sickness showed that you had sinned against God. That was another reason to stay clear.

Jesus did the opposite. He approached the sick. He touched and embraced them. He brought them back into the community, where they could find love and respect.

How about us? Do we ignore, mock, or judge some people who are ill or disabled? Or, like Jesus did with Peter's mother-in-law, do we stop, reach out a hand, and care for them? Many people in hospitals and nursing homes are praying that someone will bring them back into community by visiting them to show concern and respect. Some might even be in our own families or schools.

Take :10 Reflect

If a word or phrase from the Gospel grabs your heart, sit quietly for several minutes and repeat it to yourself, asking God to show you how it applies to your life. Or, reflect and possibly journal on one of the following questions:

- How do I react when I'm around people who are seriously ill or disabled? Who inspires me by their compassion for those who are sick?

Will You Risk Being Unclean?

Take :05 Examine

How did I live out last week's Gospel message? What was tough? What was rewarding?

Take :05 Read

A leper came to Jesus and kneeling down begged him and said, "If you wish, you can make me clean." Moved with pity, he stretched out his hand, touched him, and said to him, "I do will it. Be made clean." The leprosy left him immediately, and he was made clean. Then, warning him sternly, he dismissed him at once. He said to him, "See that you tell no one anything, but go, show yourself to the priest and offer for your cleansing what Moses prescribed; that will be proof for them." The man went away and began to publicize the whole matter. He spread the report abroad so that it was impossible for Jesus to enter a town openly. He remained outside in deserted places, and people kept coming to him from everywhere.

We see them every day—the "lepers."

They sit alone at our school lunch tables. They sit quietly in the corners of classrooms. They are the kids many look at as weird or losers. They often live "outside" the community. That is, few popular people notice them or talk to them, unless it's to make fun of them. Rarely do you see them with friends at games or parties.

They live the same fate as the lepers in Jesus' time. Scripture scholars say that the leprosy in the Gospel probably was different from the disease we call leprosy today. It was a skin condition more like psoriasis, which caused scaly, flaky skin. The worst part of the condition might have been the community's response. Ancient Judaism required lepers to live away from their families and village. They were isolated, kicked out. Jews went out of their way not to touch lepers because it made you unclean—which risked your ejection from the community as well.

But Jesus, moved by compassion, touched the leper and welcomed him back to the community, back to friends and family.

This week think about the "lepers" you pass—the people our society avoids and treats as unclean. They may be at your school or walking from shelter to shelter in your city or living in your local AIDS home. Ask for God's wisdom to know how you can bring them compassion and friendship. And be prepared for the people who will treat you as if you are unclean for doing so.

Take :10 Reflect

If a word or phrase from the Gospel grabs your heart, sit quietly for several minutes and repeat it to yourself, asking God to show you how it applies to your life. Or, reflect and possibly journal on the following question:

- How do I—or how can I— bring God's healing to the "lepers" I see in my school or community?

Seventh Sunday of Ordinary Time
Mark 2:1–12

Who Do You Know Who's Paralyzed?

Take :05 Examine

How did I live out last week's Gospel message? What was tough? What was rewarding?

Take :05 Read

When Jesus returned to Capernaum after some days, it became known that he was at home. Many gathered together so that there was no longer room for them, not even around the door, and he preached the word to them. They came bringing to him a paralytic carried by four men. Unable to get near Jesus because of the crowd, they opened up the roof above him. After they had broken through, they let down the mat on which the paralytic was lying. When Jesus saw their faith, he said to the paralytic, "Child, your sins are forgiven." Now some of the scribes were sitting there asking themselves, "Why does this man speak that way? He is blaspheming. Who but God alone can forgive sins?" Jesus immediately knew in his mind what they were thinking to themselves, so he said, "Why are you thinking such things in your hearts? Which is easier, to say to the paralytic, 'Your sins are forgiven' or to say, 'Rise, pick up your mat and walk'? But that you may know that the Son of Man has authority to forgive sins on earth"—he said to the paralytic, "I say to you, rise, pick up your mat, and go home." He rose, picked up his mat at once, and went away in the sight of everyone. They were all astounded and glorified God, saying, "We have never seen anything like this."

Carried to Jesus. Dropped down through the roof. Wow, that's service!

I wonder about those guys who carried the paralyzed man. Did they know him? Were they related? Did they have anything else to do that day? What did other people think of them?

I also wonder about the sinful habits that sometimes "paralyze" humans: greed, dishonesty, alcohol abuse, sex outside of marriage, violence. Habitual sin paralyzes by breaking relationships, damaging integrity, or even creating addictions. Habitual sin paralyzes us by stopping us from growing into the people God means us to be.

We, as Jesus' disciples, can help free friends and family members who are paralyzed by "bringing them to Jesus." We can pray for them. We can pray for the strength and wisdom to confront them about sins that are hurting them. We can ask others for help or advice about how to confront those we care about.

That is our job as disciples. It's not easy and it takes time away from other things. Some people won't like our challenge. But we'll make a difference if we try. And we *will* see some people who "pick up their mats" and break free of a sin that was hurting them.

Take :10 Reflect

If a word or phrase from the Gospel grabs your heart, sit quietly for several minutes and repeat it to yourself, asking God to show you how it applies to your life. Or, reflect and possibly journal on the following question:

- Who inspires me by his or her willingness to challenge people when they are hurting themselves or others through sin?

Eighth Sunday of Ordinary Time
Mark 2:18–22

Jesus Changes Everything

How did I live out last week's Gospel message? What was tough? What was rewarding?

The disciples of John and of the Pharisees were accustomed to fast. People came to him and objected, "Why do the disciples of John and the disciples of the Pharisees fast, but your disciples do not fast?" Jesus answered them, "Can the wedding guests fast while the bridegroom is with them? As long as they have the bridegroom with them they cannot fast. But the days will come when the bridegroom is taken away from them, and then they will fast on that day. No one sews a piece of unshrunken cloth on an old cloak. If he does, its fullness pulls away, the new from the old, and the tear gets worse. Likewise, no one pours new wine into old wineskins. Otherwise, the wine will burst the skins, and both the wine and the skins are ruined. Rather, new wine is poured into fresh wineskins."

I remember two senior girls in Las Vegas who were close friends. They enjoyed different hobbies and hung with two totally different cliques at school. There really was no reason for their friendship—except that they went on retreat together. And Jesus changes everything.

As some young friends of mine would put it, Jesus will "rock your world" if you really let him grab you. That's part of the point Jesus is making in this Gospel. Things will not be the same when you welcome Jesus into your life. God is coming to save the world through Christ and through us.

It is time to get pumped up and let that shape our life—our interests, our time, and our friendships. The closer you draw to Christ through prayer, worship, and service, the more you'll realize it's time to replace some old wineskins (habits, priorities, maybe even some friendships), because they just can't hold the new wine (Christ) that you need for a full life.

People will notice the changes. Some will be confused. Some will praise you. But some might get angry and attack you. So stay close to other Christians who also want to live and see things differently. And don't be surprised if you build some great friendships with people you never thought could be your friends. Just remember those two girls in Las Vegas.

Take :10 Reflect

If a word or phrase from the Gospel grabs your heart, sit quietly for several minutes and repeat it to yourself, asking God to show you how it applies to your life. Or, reflect and possibly journal on the following question:

- How has my relationship with Jesus changed my friendships, priorities, or habits?

First Sunday of Lent
Mark 1:12–15

Time to Choose

Take :05 Examine

How did I live out last week's Gospel message? What was tough? What was rewarding?

Take :05 Read

The Spirit drove Jesus out into the desert, and he remained in the desert for forty days, tempted by Satan. He was among wild beasts, and the angels ministered to him.

After John had been arrested, Jesus came to Galilee proclaiming the gospel of God: "This is the time of fulfillment. The kingdom of God is at hand. Repent, and believe in the gospel."

Jean Donovan was a young U.S. missionary to El Salvador in the 1980s. She worked with orphans during the nation's civil war. Government "death squads" often threatened her and other Catholic missionaries because of their work with the poor.

Several friends urged Jean to come home because of the violence. She thought about it, but refused. Who would care for the children, she wrote in her last letter, if she left? Jean, a devout Catholic, had made her choice.

Soldiers murdered her soon after that.

Lent is the time to reflect and make choices. That's why Jesus went to the desert. He went to commit to what his life was going to be about. He needed time away to think and pray. In the end, like Jean Donovan, he chose to stand for God's compassion and justice, even though that got his cousin, John the Baptist, arrested.

We need Lent. We need time away to realize that our lives can make a difference. We need time to face those "demons" that draw us away from using our lives for God to heal the world. Will I be a person who forgives or one who gets even? Will I spend my life seeking power and wealth or in serving others? Will I take risks in order to do the right thing?

Join Jesus in the desert this Lent. Add time to your daily prayer. Make a weekly service commitment. Look honestly at your strengths and weaknesses. Ask Jean Donovan, now with the saints in heaven, to pray for you as you look honestly at the choices you face.

Take :10 Reflect

If a word or phrase from the Gospel grabs your heart, sit quietly for several minutes and repeat it to yourself, asking God to show you how it applies to your life. Or, reflect and possibly journal on the following question:

- How can I add more prayer or service to my life this Lent, as part of my trip to the desert with Jesus?

We're in Good Company

Take :05 Examine

How did I live out last week's Gospel message? What was tough? What was rewarding?

Take :05 Read

Jesus took Peter, James, and John and led them up a high mountain apart by themselves. And he was transfigured before them, and his clothes became dazzling white, such as no fuller on earth could bleach them. Then Elijah appeared to them along with Moses, and they were conversing with Jesus. Then Peter said to Jesus in reply, "Rabbi, it is good that we are here! Let us make three tents: one for you, one for Moses, and one for Elijah." He hardly knew what to say, they were so terrified. Then a cloud came, casting a shadow over them; from the cloud came a voice, "This is my beloved Son. Listen to him." Suddenly, looking around, they no longer saw anyone but Jesus alone with them.

As they were coming down from the mountain, he charged them not to relate what they had seen to anyone, except when the Son of Man had risen from the dead. So they kept the matter to themselves, questioning what rising from the dead meant.

If we get confused sometimes about what God wants, we're in good company.

This week a few of the Apostles join Jesus on a mountain, where he is transfigured. That is, Jesus is transformed so they see who he really is. They hear God's voice telling them to listen to Jesus' words.

Then they go down the mountain and still are confused. Later they even abandon Jesus.

The Apostles were human like us. It would be nice if we always saw God and heard God's voice so clearly. But it just doesn't happen that way. God at times can seem close, and at other times distant. The Scriptures can seem clear at times, but then confusing at other times when you try to live them in daily life. Some of us have had "transfiguration" experiences, like powerful retreats where everything seems so clear or moments of prayer when God seems so close. But even our greatest saints have talked about how hard it is to hold on to that clarity.

What did the Apostles do when they were confused? The Scriptures tell us that they kept trying. They prayed and read Scripture together. They prayed before decisions. Then they did their best and trusted that the Holy Spirit would work through them. And in the end, they changed the world.

Take :10 Reflect

If a word or phrase from the Gospel grabs your heart, sit quietly for several minutes and repeat it to yourself, asking God to show you how it applies to your life. Or, reflect and possibly journal on the following question:

- Where do I turn when I'm confused about my faith or about how to grow close to God?

Just Lose It Sometimes!

Take :05 Examine

How did I live out last week's Gospel message? What was tough? What was rewarding?

Take :05 Read

Since the Passover of the Jews was near, Jesus went up to Jerusalem. He found in the temple area those who sold oxen, sheep, and doves, as well as the money changers seated there. He made a whip out of cords and drove them all out of the temple area, with the sheep and oxen, and spilled the coins of the money changers and overturned their tables, and to those who sold doves he said, "Take these out of here, and stop making my Father's house a marketplace." His disciples recalled the words of Scripture, Zeal for your house will consume me. *At this the Jews answered and said to him, "What sign can you show us for doing this?" Jesus answered and said to them, "Destroy this temple and in three days I will raise it up."* The Jews said, "This temple has been under construction for forty-six years, and you will raise it up in three days?" *But he was speaking about the temple of his body. Therefore, when he was raised from the dead, his disciples remembered that he had said this, and they came to believe the Scripture and the word Jesus had spoken.* (John 2:13–22)

He loved people so much, he sometimes just lost it.

This was the situation. Faithful Jews coming to the temple for worship first had to buy animals for sacrifice and exchange their coins for those that would be acceptable for their temple tax. But some Scripture scholars say the people selling the animals and changing the money were making a making a huge profit because people had to deal with them. They had a monopoly.

Some scholars say this infuriated Jesus. He saw a system set up to take advantage of good people coming to worship their God. The system especially hurt poor people. It was an example of how the religious and political leaders of Jesus' time abused people.

Getting angry over injustices isn't unchristian—but it doesn't have to lead to violence. Martin Luther King Jr. is a perfect example. He fought racism with righteous anger, but never used violence or threats of it against his opponents.

The closer you grow to Jesus, the more you'll become angry when you see people—especially the outcasts—ignored or abused. Use that anger as fuel to stand up nonviolently for people. Speak for kids at school who are put down. Refuse to back away from our society's outcasts, like poor people or people with AIDS. Join with other Catholic activists when they mobilize for peace or pro-life issues. But always remember Jesus' other words, "Love your enemies," even while you oppose their actions.

Just think how much the world will change when more Christians lose it over injustices like Jesus did.

Take :10 Reflect

If a word or phrase from the Gospel grabs your heart, sit quietly for several minutes and repeat it to yourself, asking God to show you how it applies to your life. Or, reflect and possibly journal on the following questions:

- What injustices anger you? What are you doing about them?

Jesus Saves; We Condemn

Take :05 Examine

How did I live out last week's Gospel message? What was tough? What was rewarding?

Take :05 Read

Jesus said to Nicodemus: "Just as Moses lifted up the serpent in the desert, so must the Son of Man be lifted up, so that everyone who believes in him may have eternal life."

For God so loved the world that he gave his only Son, so that everyone who believes in him might not perish but might have eternal life. For God did not send his Son into the world to condemn the world, but that the world might be saved through him. Whoever believes in him will not be condemned, but whoever does not believe has already been condemned, because he has not believed in the name of the only Son of God. And this is the verdict, that the light came into the world, but people preferred darkness to light, because their works were evil. For everyone who does wicked things hates the light and does not come toward the light, so that his works might not be exposed. But whoever lives the truth comes to the light, so that his works may be clearly seen as done in God.

When I was a young man just out of graduate school, I felt condemned.

I was successful in my career, but empty on the inside. Despite all my hard work, life seemed meaningless. I worked hard in college, but not at being a Christian. In fact, I fell away from God in college. I stopped going to church. I never prayed or read the Bible. I didn't even think about serving people who suffered.

You see, I condemned myself—to a self-centered, Godless life that felt empty because it was so empty.

Sometimes we think God is busy watching for opportunities to condemn us. But Jesus clears up all that in today's Gospel. God doesn't look for opportunities to condemn us, but to save us from lives without meaning and to save us for life eternal. We condemn ourselves if we ignore Jesus' recipe for living. Through sin and selfishness, we can build our own prison.

But God wants to free us. So God sent Jesus to show us the way. Isn't it great to know that God's only desire is for us to live full lives now and into eternity? And even if we spend most of our life looking in the wrong places, God never withdraws the offer of salvation.

Eventually I took the Lord up on the offer and decided to follow Jesus and shine his light for the world. And since then I've been free.

Take :10 Reflect

If a word or phrase from the Gospel grabs your heart, sit quietly for several minutes and repeat it to yourself, asking God to show you how it applies to your life. Or, reflect and possibly journal on the following question:

- Do you have any sinful habits that are slowly condemning you? If so, talk to God this week about finding help to break them.

Let Your Fear Die

Take :05 Examine

How did I live out last week's Gospel message? What was tough? What was rewarding?

Take :05 Read

Some Greeks who had come to worship at the Passover Feast came to Philip, who was from Bethsaida in Galilee, and asked him, "Sir, we would like to see Jesus." Philip went and told Andrew; then Andrew and Philip went and told Jesus. Jesus answered them, "The hour has come for the Son of Man to be glorified. Amen, amen, I say to you, unless a grain of wheat falls to the ground and dies, it remains just a grain of wheat; but if it dies, it produces much fruit. Whoever loves his life loses it, and whoever hates his life in this world will preserve it for eternal life. Whoever serves me must follow me, and where I am, there also will my servant be. The Father will honor whoever serves me.

"I am troubled now. Yet what should I say? 'Father, save me from this hour'? But it was for this purpose that I came to this hour. Father, glorify your name." Then a voice came from heaven, "I have glorified it and will glorify it again." The crowd there heard it and said it was thunder; but others said, "An angel has spoken to him." Jesus answered and said, "This voice did not come for my sake but for yours. Now is the time of judgment on this world; now the ruler of this world will be driven out. And when I am lifted up from the earth, I will draw everyone to myself." He said this indicating the kind of death he would die.

I remember the first time I volunteered at an overnight shelter. I was scared.

Were these guys dangerous? Would I say something to tick them off? I only went because a good friend who had gone many times before went with me. And am I grateful that I went.

I found out I had nothing to fear. And that first shelter trip started an incredible journey. That was more than fifteen years ago. Since then I've worked at countless shelters in the United States and Mexico. I've met incredible people. Some have been homeless. Some have been volunteers. If I hadn't conquered my fears that first night, I'd have missed so much.

God has incredible experiences lined up for you. God has awesome people ready to enrich your life. You only need to follow Jesus' advice this week to find it all. Abandon the world's measure for happiness. Go where Jesus would go. Find the people who are forgotten or abused. Serve till it hurts—and then serve some more. Give up time you'd rather use for yourself. That's what it means to be like the grain of wheat.

Don't let fear stop you. It didn't stop Jesus. Reach out in prayer for courage. Do the right thing in spite of pressure. You'll find a new life you never expected—and it will be awesome.

Take :10 Reflect

If a word or phrase from the Gospel grabs your heart, sit quietly for several minutes, repeating it to yourself and asking God to show you how it applies to your life. Or, reflect and possibly journal on the following question:

- How does fear sometimes limit teen disciples from living the Gospel?

Palm Sunday (The Passion)
Mark 14:1—15:47 or Mark 15:1–39

Don't Miss a Moment This Week

Take :05 Examine

How did I live out last week's Gospel message? What was tough? What was rewarding?

Take :05 Read

Then they crucified him and divided his garments by casting lots to see what each should take. It was nine o'clock in the morning when they crucified him. The inscription of the charge against him read, "The King of the Jews." . . .

At noon darkness came over the whole land until three in the afternoon. And at three o'clock Jesus cried out in a loud voice, "Eloi, Eloi, lema sabachthani?" which is translated, "My God, my God, why have you forsaken me?" Some of the bystanders who heard it said, "Look, he is calling Elijah." One of them ran, soaked a sponge in wine, put it on a reed and gave it to him to drink, saying, "Wait, let us see if Elijah comes to take him down." Jesus gave a loud cry and breathed his last.

The veil of the sanctuary was torn in two from top to bottom. When the centurion who stood facing him saw how he breathed his last he said, "Truly this man was the Son of God!" (Mark 15:24–26,33–39)

Courage. Honor. Integrity.
Fear. Abandonment. Persecution.
Victory.

It all happens between Palm Sunday and Holy Saturday. One man, determined to change the world, stands with honor and integrity as others humiliate and insult him. He

56

chooses nonviolence while others beat and torture him. With his last breath, he forgives instead of curses.

Walk with this man this week. On Thursday watch him kneel and wash feet. Think about how he has served you and where you can serve others in his name. On Friday watch him stand with dignity against the forces of violence and oppression. Think about his sacrifice and ask for his strength to stand peacefully but forcefully for all those who are crucified by rejection, poverty, or oppression in our schools, cities, and world. On Saturday listen to all the readings at Mass. They tell of God's repeated attempts, since the beginning of time, to save us. Give your life anew to that God, and ask how you can help save God's world.

Don't miss this week. All you need to know about your life unfolds in the life of one man who decided two thousand years ago to change the world.

Take :10 Reflect

If a word or phrase from the Gospel grabs your heart, sit quietly for several minutes and repeat it to yourself, asking God to show you how it applies to your life. Or, reflect and possibly journal on the following question:

• How can I shape my schedule so that I can attend Church on Holy Thursday, Good Friday, and Holy Saturday?

He Is Risen! Just Look Around!

Take :05 Examine

How did I live out last week's Gospel message? What was tough? What was rewarding?

Take :05 Read

On the first day of the week, Mary of Magdala came to the tomb early in the morning, while it was still dark, and saw the stone removed from the tomb. So she ran and went to Simon Peter and to the other disciple whom Jesus loved, and told them, "They have taken the Lord from the tomb, and we don't know where they put him." So Peter and the other disciple went out and came to the tomb. They both ran, but the other disciple ran faster than Peter and arrived at the tomb first; he bent down and saw the burial cloths there, but did not go in. When Simon Peter arrived after him, he went into the tomb and saw the burial cloths there, and the cloth that had covered his head, not with the burial cloths but rolled up in a separate place. Then the other disciple also went in, the one who had arrived at the tomb first, and he saw and believed. For they did not yet understand the Scripture that he had to rise from the dead.

I believe Jesus has risen. Why? Because I've seen the evidence:

- I know Ryan, a former student of mine, who rode a bike from San Francisco to Washington, D.C., to urge Catholics to help poor people.

- When I call out for help in prayer, I find peace, hope, or answers within myself or from someone who brings them into my life.

- I've worked with countless teens who have given up countless hours to lead retreats that urge their friends to meet, follow, and love Jesus Christ.

I could go on.

I didn't see Jesus leave the cave. I've only heard stories. But the disciple in the Gospel who reached the tomb first didn't see him leave either. He only saw the empty tomb. He believed because of other evidence. Maybe he believed because he saw the way Jesus changed the world while he lived. Maybe he believed because he saw the difference Jesus' disciples made when they followed his recipe for life.

You never saw Jesus leave the cave. But look around. There is plenty of evidence for the Resurrection. Look in the Scriptures and reach out to other Christians for help with a problem, and you'll find guidance from Jesus, who still lives today through them. Live like the role models who have inspired you by their Christian lives, and you'll find happiness by following the living Jesus. Follow that nudge in your conscience to help others, and you'll be an active participant in Jesus' Resurrection by changing the world.

Yes, there's plenty of evidence that Christ is alive and still changing the world. For those who are actively living their faith, it is hard to miss.

Take :10 Reflect

If a word or phrase from the Gospel grabs your heart, sit quietly for several minutes and repeat it to yourself, asking God to show you how it applies to your life. Or, reflect and possibly journal on the following questions:

- What or who are the signs in your life that Jesus has risen and is alive in the world? What actions might you take so that you can more readily see those signs?

Don't Miss Out Like Thomas

Take :05 Examine

How did I live out last week's Gospel message? What was tough? What was rewarding?

Take :05 Read

On the evening of that first day of the week, when the doors were locked, where the disciples were, for fear of the Jews, Jesus came and stood in their midst and said to them, "Peace be with you." When he had said this, he showed them his hands and his side. The disciples rejoiced when they saw the Lord. Jesus said to them again, "Peace be with you. As the Father has sent me, so I send you." And when he had said this, he breathed on them and said to them, "Receive the Holy Spirit. Whose sins you forgive are forgiven them, and whose sins you retain are retained."

Thomas, called Didymus, one of the Twelve, was not with them when Jesus came. So the other disciples said to him, "We have seen the Lord." But he said to them, "Unless I see the mark of the nails in his hands and put my finger into the nailmarks and put my hand into his side, I will not believe."

Now a week later his disciples were again inside and Thomas was with them. Jesus came, although the doors were locked, and stood in their midst and said, "Peace be with you." Then he said to Thomas, "Put your finger here and see my hands, and bring your hand and put it into my side, and do not be unbelieving, but believe." Thomas answered and said to him, "My Lord and my God!" Jesus said to him, "Have you come to believe because you have seen me? Blessed are those who have not seen and have believed." (John 20:19–29)

"I can be a Christian without going to church." I've heard it many times from teens and adults. And I've always disagreed.

Why? Because of Thomas.

Thomas was gone when Jesus appeared to the Apostles. Then he had trouble believing when the Apostles told him about it. He only believed when he saw Jesus with them.

The message? We need Christian community to really believe in the Resurrection. It's the community that gives us the strength, challenge, and guidance to act as we believe.

Notice that Jesus gave the Apostles peace and a mission while they were gathered. The same is true today. It is in Christian community—Mass, service trips, youth groups, religion classes, retreats, even phone calls to Christian friends—that we most fully find Christ's peace, remember our mission, and receive strength to act as we believe. If we never worship, never talk about our faith, or never serve with other Catholics, pretty soon we'll find it harder to believe. And our actions might not show that we believe in a savior who calls us to live radically different lives because he rose from the dead.

Take :10 Reflect

If a word or phrase from the Gospel grabs your heart, sit quietly for several minutes and repeat it to yourself, and ask God to show you how it applies to your life. Or, reflect and possibly journal on the following question:

- What type of Christian gathering (Mass, youth groups, retreats, service trips, phone conversations) helps me the most to connect with the Christian community, and why?

Take the Stand and Witness!

Take :05 Examine

How did I live out last week's Gospel message? What was tough? What was rewarding?

Take :05 Read

The two disciples recounted what had taken place on the way, and how Jesus was made known to them in the breaking of the bread.

While they were still speaking about this, he stood in their midst and said to them, "Peace be with you." But they were startled and terrified and thought that they were seeing a ghost. Then he said to them, "Why are you troubled? And why do questions arise in your hearts? Look at my hands and my feet, that it is I myself. Touch me and see, because a ghost does not have flesh and bones as you can see I have." And as he said this, he showed them his hands and his feet. While they were still incredulous for joy and were amazed, he asked them, "Have you anything here to eat?" They gave him a piece of baked fish; he took it and ate it in front of them.

He said to them, "These are my words that I spoke to you while I was still with you, that everything written about me in the law of Moses and in the prophets and psalms must be fulfilled." Then he opened their minds to understand the Scriptures. (Luke 24:35–45)

Witnesses to the Resurrection? Yeah, I've met them, especially in the hospital.

There was the patient with extreme hip pain who prayed for the people with more serious medical problems.

There was the older patient who almost died but said she doesn't fear death because Christ had comforted her in prayer. There was the patient with cancer who was looking for a parish to join because he always kept "Jesus in my heart"—even though he felt rejected by the Church in the past.

I look back on the faith of those folks and I say, "Christ is risen!"

Are you a convincing witness to others?

That is this Gospel's challenge. Your faith might be the only "Gospel" that some people read. They'll read it in how you treat friends, family, and even enemies. They'll read it in your attitude toward poor people. They'll read it in how you use money and choose goals.

That's heavy stuff. We aren't perfect, and we mess up a lot. But don't worry. More than anything else, people will see the Gospel alive when you apologize, admit your failings, and start over.

You're a sinner. So am I. But we're still called to witness to the Resurrection by passing the Gospel with our generation and down to the next generation. The Apostles took Jesus up on that. And the word has spread from generation to generation for two thousand years now. It's now partly on your shoulders. But God put it there because God has so much faith in you.

Take :10 Reflect

If a word or phrase from the Gospel grabs your heart, sit quietly for several minutes and repeat it to yourself, asking God to show you how it applies to your life. Or, reflect and possibly journal on the following question:

- As I review what typically happens in my daily routine, where do I have opportunities to witness to the Resurrection by my faith in action?

Hey, You! There's Some Sheep Looking For You!

Take :05 Examine

How did I live out last week's Gospel message? What was tough? What was rewarding?

Take :05 Read

Jesus said: "I am the good shepherd. A good shepherd lays down his life for the sheep. A hired man, who is not a shepherd and whose sheep are not his own, sees a wolf coming and leaves the sheep and runs away, and the wolf catches and scatters them. This is because he works for pay and has no concern for the sheep. I am the good shepherd, and I know mine and mine know me, just as the Father knows me and I know the Father; and I will lay down my life for the sheep. I have other sheep that do not belong to this fold. These also I must lead, and they will hear my voice, and there will be one flock, one shepherd. This is why the Father loves me, because I lay down my life in order to take it up again. No one takes it from me, but I lay it down on my own. I have power to lay it down, and power to take it up again. This command I have received from my Father."

It happens after almost every teen retreat or teen-led youth-group meeting.

Teen leaders stand in awe. They can't believe that other teens actually found help with their lives and their faith by listening to the teen leaders' talks. In other words, they can't believe that teens have the power to be "good shepherds."

Too often we only think about Jesus when we think about the good shepherd. But that misses a big part of Jesus' message. He came to teach us about shepherding, and he left us a flock to tend. He told us to call on the Spirit when we need extra strength or wisdom for the job.

Think for a moment about sheep. Think about how vulnerable they were in Jesus' time. Wolves could attack. Thieves could steal them. They needed food and drink.

Think for a moment about people today—teens and adults. Like wolves, commercials prey on many who believe they are worthless unless they are beautiful. Like thieves, drugs and alcohol steal many people's lives away with promises of pleasure and escape. Like hunger, loneliness and isolation starve those who don't know where to turn for someone who will care. And finally, many thirst for a message they can count on in a world that is so filled with disappointments.

It seems like we need plenty of good shepherds. You have the power to protect, to feed, to save people—teens and adults. Take leadership in our Church, in a youth group, a retreat program, or a service trip. Trust *the* Good Shepherd; he'll show you how to do it all. And like so many other teens I've met, you'll eventually stand back awed by the difference you've made.

Take :10 Reflect

If a word or phrase from the Gospel grabs your heart, sit quietly for several minutes and repeat it to yourself, asking God to show you how it applies to your life. Or, reflect and possibly journal on the following question:

- How have I made a difference—or how can I make a differ-ence—by showing leadership in my Church or my school?

You Are Connected!

Take :05 Examine

How did I live out last week's Gospel message? What was tough? What was rewarding?

Take :05 Read

Jesus said to his disciples: "I am the true vine, and my Father is the vine grower. He takes away every branch in me that does not bear fruit, and every one that does he prunes so that it bears more fruit. You are already pruned because of the word that I spoke to you. Remain in me, as I remain in you. Just as a branch cannot bear fruit on its own unless it remains on the vine, so neither can you unless you remain in me. I am the vine, you are the branches. Whoever remains in me and I in him will bear much fruit, because without me you can do nothing. Anyone who does not remain in me will be thrown out like a branch and wither; people will gather them and throw them into a fire and they will be burned. If you remain in me and my words remain in you, ask for whatever you want and it will be done for you. By this is my Father glorified, that you bear much fruit and become my disciples."

Let me tell you about a high school freshman who quit football because he lacked confidence and didn't have friends on the team. He later regretted it. But it was too hard for him, with all his self-doubts, to practice each day.

Confidence and friendship. Both can be tough to find. Many teens struggle to connect with peers who will accept them as they are. Many also struggle to be confident in who they are.

This week's Gospel hits home on both points. Even though all of us—teens and adults—can feel alone and insecure, it reminds us that in some mystical but real way, we are always connected to Jesus. And through that connection, we can discover and develop our talents for changing the world. We also can use that connection to call for help when we feel disconnected and lonely.

Let me tell you about another freshman. He was a shy, insecure kid. But during high school, he connected with Jesus through service trips and retreats. Through them he became a confident leader, well respected by his classmates, with strong friendships.

You're a teen. You'll probably struggle with confidence and loneliness. But during those times, reread this passage. And remember, you're connected to the Savior of the world. Like any relationship, the more you hang out with Jesus, the stronger the connection becomes. So hang out with him by involving yourself in Mass, religion class, prayer, and friendships with other Christians. You'll feel the connection growing. And the more you strengthen that connection, the easier it will be to find the friends and the confidence you've hoped for.

Take :10 Reflect

If a word or phrase from the Gospel grabs your heart, sit quietly for several minutes and repeat it to yourself, asking God to show you how it applies to your life. Or, reflect and possibly journal on the following questions:

- Who do you know at school or in your Church that is lonely? Jesus wants them connected to friendship. What could you do to ease their loneliness?

Don't Like 'Em, *Love* 'Em

Take :05 Examine

How did I live out last week's Gospel message? What was tough? What was rewarding?

Take :05 Read

Jesus said to his disciples: "As the Father loves me, so I also love you. Remain in my love. If you keep my commandments, you will remain in my love, just as I have kept my Father's commandments and remain in his love.

"I have told you this so that my joy may be in you and your joy may be complete. This is my commandment: love one another as I love you. No one has greater love than this, to lay down one's life for one's friends. You are my friends if you do what I command you. I no longer call you slaves, because a slave does not know what his master is doing. I have called you friends, because I have told you everything I have heard from my Father. It was not you who chose me, but I who chose you and appointed you to go and bear fruit that will remain, so that whatever you ask the Father in my name he may give you. This I command you: love one another."

It was a long time before I realized that you don't have to like every Christian.

I've met a lot of Christians with whom I never want to be friends. Our personalities clash. And I'm sure I've driven some of them crazy.

But eventually I realized that "liking" and "loving" are totally different. We like our friends. We like people with personalities that mesh with ours. Liking is easy. It kind of comes naturally.

But Jesus, in this week's Gospel, pleads with his disciples to love one another as he loves them. Jesus wants members of his community to sacrifice for each other and the world—even if they aren't friends and have trouble getting along. That means listening to others' opinions, putting their needs ahead of yours, putting disagreements or personality clashes aside, and focusing on your common tie—the Christian mission to make the world a better place, especially for poor people.

That can be tough. You might have to lead a retreat with someone with whom you've had several conflicts. You might have to do service with people who share none of your other interests. That's why Jesus tells us to ask God for whatever we need. God's power can help us love Christians that we have trouble liking or with whom we have conflicts. The Holy Spirit can show us where we are connected, despite our differences, and how we can work together for God's Kingdom.

Remember, we are Jesus' friends when we follow his commandments, not our own likes and dislikes. And this fractured world desperately needs to see Christians sacrifice for one another—regardless of their differences or conflicts—in a common mission to change the world.

Take :10 Reflect

If a word or phrase from the Gospel grabs your heart, sit quietly for several minutes and repeat it to yourself, asking God to show you how it applies to your life. Or, reflect and possibly journal on the following question:

- Whom am I being called to love, even though I don't yet like the person?

Create a World to Change the World

Take :05 Examine

How did I live out last week's Gospel message? What was tough? What was rewarding?

Take :05 Read

Lifting his eyes to heaven, Jesus prayed, saying: "Holy Father, keep them in your name that you have given me, so that they may be one just as we are. When I was with them I protected them in your name that you gave me, and I guarded them, and none of them was lost except the son of destruction, in order that the Scripture might be fulfilled. But now I am coming to you. I speak this in the world so that they may share my joy completely. I gave them your word, and the world hated them, because they do not belong to the world any more than I belong to the world. I do not ask that you take them out of the world but that you keep them from the evil one. They do not belong to the world any more than I belong to the world. Consecrate them in the truth. Your word is truth. As you sent me into the world, so I sent them into the world. And I consecrate myself for them, so that they also may be consecrated in truth."

When I worked in a high school, we used to gather our student retreat leaders for lunch discussions about the ups and downs of living what they were preaching. It wasn't easy for them. That's why they needed to get together. Over lunch they'd talk and pray, laugh and gripe, listen and think.

The lunches helped them create a world within *the* world. They created a Christian world where they found support for choosing reconciliation over vengeance, service over selfishness, and honesty over deceit. Peer pressure is a tough thing to fight— for adults and teens. Many people abandon living their faith openly or define it as unrealistic because they get so much flak from friends, family, classmates, and coworkers.

Jesus prays in this week's Gospel for his disciples because he knows how the world will wear them down, even though they've all come to know and love him. Jesus knows that without God working 24-7 to protect them, they'll soon forget all they learned from him.

You can create a "world within *the* world" by gathering with other Christians. Go to a youth group. Start a prayer and discussion meeting. Commit to regular service trips with friends. Share your opinions and listen to others in religion class. Or just call a Christian friend regularly for an honest talk about life. Within this Christian world, you'll find the strength and protection Jesus asked God to send. You'll find greater strength to stand for Christ in the larger world when the going gets tough.

Take :10 Reflect

If a word or phrase from the Gospel grabs your heart, sit quietly for several minutes and repeat it to yourself, asking God to show you how it applies to your life. Or, reflect and possibly journal on the following question:

- Identify two or three strategies you could follow for creating a Christian world within your larger world.

Catch *This* Spirit

Take :05 Examine

How did I live out last week's Gospel message? What was tough? What was rewarding?

Take :05 Read

On the evening of that first day of the week, when the doors were locked, where the disciples were, for fear of the Jews, Jesus came and stood in their midst and said to them, "Peace be with you." When he had said this, he showed them his hands and his side. The disciples rejoiced when they saw the Lord. Jesus said to them again, "Peace be with you. As the Father has sent me, so I send you." And when he had said this, he breathed on them and said to them, "Receive the Holy Spirit. Whose sins you forgive are forgiven them, and whose sins you retain are retained."

When I think of the Holy Spirit, I think of Bill's death.

Bill was a teen in our parish youth group when he died tragically. His death shook me up so much that I wasn't sure I could minister to his friends and family. So I prayed for God to help me help them.

After prayer, I remembered that a good friend, a priest, was in town visiting. So I tracked him down. We went for a walk. We talked about Bill's death. I cried some. We prayed.

Later I drove to the funeral home, knowing God needed me to be there for Bill's friends and family. As I pulled into the parking lot, a calm feeling spread through me. I went into the wake confident that I could bring some of God's peace with me to share. The Holy Spirit was with me. I connected with the Spirit by praying for strength to do

God's will and by following the inspiration to connect with my priest friend.

The Holy Spirit is alive in our Church. It directs us when we seek guidance. It calms us when we face crisis. It strengthens us to be peace amid the world's pain. In this week's Gospel, Jesus gives that Spirit to his first followers. And Christian community is still where we find it. We find the Spirit when we get together with other Christians to talk and pray about our joys and fears. The Spirit continually seeks to bring us together to guide us, strengthen us, and send us. You have encountered this Spirit. Take time this week to think about when and where.

Take :10 Reflect

If a word or phrase from the Gospel grabs your heart, sit quietly for several minutes and repeat it to yourself, asking God to show you how it applies to your life. Or, reflect and possibly journal on the following question:

- Recall a time when you've felt strengthened, guided, or inspired to act after meeting with one or more Christians.

Go Beyond Your Comfort Zone

Take :05 Examine

How did I live out last week's Gospel message? What was tough? What was rewarding?

Take :05 Read

The eleven disciples went to Galilee, to the mountain to which Jesus had ordered them. When they all saw him, they worshiped, but they doubted. Then Jesus approached and said to them, "All power in heaven and on earth has been given to me. Go, therefore, and make disciples of all nations, baptizing them in the name of the Father, and of the Son, and of the Holy Spirit, teaching them to observe all that I have commanded you. And behold, I am with you always, until the end of the age."

That was a shock to Jesus' first followers. Go to *all* nations? But they were Jews!

Nonetheless, that was Matthew's message for early Christians. The Gospel was originally written for a community of mostly Jewish followers of Jesus. Go beyond your comfort zone, it tells them. Build relationships with people who are different, with people you never expected to enter your life.

Does that shock you? Look around at your life. Is everyone the same? Same skin color? Same interests? Same economic level? Same school activities? It's easy for us humans to stay in our comfort zone. But if we do, we miss out.

Jesus grew up in Galilee, which some scholars argue was an ethnically mixed part of Israel. His Apostles were also quite a mix. One wanted to start a revolution against the

Romans (Simon the Zealot) while another collected taxes for them (Matthew). In this Gospel, which is the climax of the Gospel of Matthew, Jesus sends this diverse group from a diverse area to baptize all people.

The message is clear. We find life more full when we meet, serve, learn from, and develop relationships with all types of people. I am a white, middle-class man. I've learned a lot about sacrifice and faith from Mexican friends who have worked hard to build a life in the United States. I've learned about prejudice from gay and black friends. I've learned about compassion by listening to homeless people worry about their homeless friends.

Here' some ideas for you. When you go to soup kitchens or shelters, take time to talk with the people who eat or sleep there. Eat lunch or mix during parties with classmates who have different interests. Ask classmates with different ethnic or religious backgrounds to tell you a little bit about their culture. Get some friends together and go to a local ethnic festival. Or have lunch or coffee in a neighborhood that's different ethnically or economically from your own. Maybe you'll meet someone new there. Look for programs or retreats that help teens get to know teens from different countries, races, or religions. Search the Internet for sites that explore different cultures.

Just leave the borders behind. Stretch yourself.

Take :10 Reflect

If a word or phrase from the Gospel grabs your heart, sit quietly for several minutes and repeat it to yourself, asking God to show you how it applies to your life. Or, reflect and possibly journal on the following questions:

- What are some of the benefits you could receive from building relationships with people who have different interests, cultures, or economic backgrounds? How might you go about building those relationships?

Be What You Eat!

How did I live out last week's Gospel message? What was tough? What was rewarding?

On the first day of the Feast of Unleavened Bread, when they sacrificed the Passover lamb, Jesus' disciples said to him, "Where do you want us to go and prepare for you to eat the Passover?" He sent two of his disciples and said to them, "Go into the city and a man will meet you, carrying a jar of water. Follow him. Wherever he enters, say to the master of the house, 'The Teacher says, "Where is my guest room where I may eat the Passover with my disciples?"' Then he will show you a large upper room furnished and ready. Make the preparations for us there." The disciples then went off, entered the city, and found it just as he had told them; and they prepared the Passover.

While they were eating, he took bread, said the blessing, broke it, gave it to them, and said, "Take it; this is my body." Then he took a cup, gave thanks, and gave it to them, and they all drank from it. He said to them, "This is my blood of the covenant, which will be shed for many." (Mark 14:12–16,22–24)

Archbishop Oscar Romero became what he ate.

He was an archbishop who spoke out boldly for human rights during El Salvador's civil war. During the war the military killed many lay Catholics, sisters, and priests because they helped the poor. Unfortunately, during that time the U.S. government funded the Salvadoran military.

Archbishop Romero met the same fate in 1980 when a soldier shot him during Mass. So during his last Mass, this man who had consecrated and received the body of Christ so many times, fully became the body of Christ by dying for God's Kingdom.

Are you what you eat?

Each time we receive Christ's body and blood in Communion, we ask God to make us Christ's body and blood. We agree to stand for the powerless and forgive those who've harmed us, regardless of the cost. Take Sue as an example. She's a teen I know who serves homeless people and her parish as a way to live out the Eucharist. It takes time she could spend on herself. Some people think its nuts to help poor people. But as she matures, she is becoming what she eats.

This all started when Jesus shared bread and wine with his Apostles and then gave his life. The Apostles continued breaking bread, sharing the cup, and giving their lives. The cycle has continued to this day and includes all those ordinary Christians you know who give themselves as "bread" to people who need them.

It's not magic. We'll still make a lot of mistakes. But the connection is clear. This week during Communion, ask for new strength to be what you eat.

Take :10 Reflect

If a word or phrase from the Gospel grabs your heart, sit quietly for several minutes and repeat it to yourself, asking God to show you how it applies to your life. Or, reflect and possibly journal on the following question:

- What biblical characters, saints, or people you know inspire you to "become what you eat" and live the sacrificial love of Jesus?

Ninth Sunday of Ordinary Time
Mark 2:23—3:6 or Mark 2:23–28

Don't "Rule" Out Compassion

Take :05 Examine

How did I live out last week's Gospel message? What was tough? What was rewarding?

Take :05 Read

As Jesus was passing through a field of grain on the sabbath, his disciples began to make a path while picking the heads of grain. At this the Pharisees said to him, "Look, why are they doing what is unlawful on the sabbath?" He said to them, "Have you never read what David did when he was in need and he and his companions were hungry? How he went into the house of God when Abiathar was high priest and ate the bread of offering that only the priests could lawfully eat, and shared it with his companions?" Then he said to them, "The sabbath was made for man, not man for the sabbath. That is why the Son of Man is lord even of the sabbath."

Again he entered the synagogue. There was a man there who had a withered hand. They watched him closely to see if he would cure him on the sabbath so that they might accuse him. He said to the man with the withered hand, "Come up here before us." Then he said to them, "Is it lawful to do good on the sabbath rather than to do evil, to save life rather than to destroy it?" But they remained silent. Looking around at them with anger and grieved at their hardness of heart, he said to the man, "Stretch out your hand." He stretched it out and his hand was restored. (Mark 2:23—3:5)

When I was a kid, I was often afraid that God was going to catch me.

I saw God as a bookkeeper, always keeping close count of my mistakes, or as a judge, waiting to punish me if I broke the rules. Because of that, I often did good things more out of fear of God rather than out of love for God.

Jesus, in this Gospel, shows me again how wrong I was about God. Our God isn't watching for our missteps. Our God is focused instead on helping each of us where we need it the most. Our God doesn't enforce rules. Our God responds with compassion when we need help.

The Pharisees had a different image of God. One Scripture scholar says that they believed Jews needed to follow more than six hundred different rules to keep God's favor. Jesus' image of God—a God who cared less about rules and more about helping others—was such a threat to the Pharisees that they plotted to kill Jesus.

Take time this week to think about your image of God. Do you understand God as being more focused on mercy and love or on rules? Do you see the connection between some Christian rules for living and God's compassion? How do you reflect God's image to others? Do you let compassion guide your relationships with friends, classmates, teammates, and family—even when it's not convenient?

Take :10 Reflect

If a word or phrase from the Gospel grabs your heart, sit quietly for several minutes and repeat it to yourself, asking God to show you how it applies to your life. Or, reflect and possibly journal on one of the following questions:

- How has your image of God changed since grade school? Whom do you admire for her or his compassion?

Enlarge Your Family

Take :05 Examine

How did I live out last week's Gospel message? What was tough? What was rewarding?

Take :05 Read

Jesus came home with his disciples. Again the crowd gathered, making it impossible for them even to eat. When his relatives heard of this they set out to seize him, for they said, "He is out of his mind." The scribes who had come from Jerusalem said, "He is possessed by Beelzebul," and "By the prince of demons he drives out demons." . . .

His mother and his brothers arrived. Standing outside they sent word to him and called him. A crowd seated around him told him, "Your mother and your brothers and your sisters are outside asking for you." But he said to them in reply, "Who are my mother and my brothers?" And looking around at those seated in the circle he said, "Here are my mother and my brothers. For whoever does the will of God is my brother and sister and mother." (Mark 3:20–22,31–35)

During the war in Iraq, I knew some religious sisters who wore buttons that read, "I have family in Iraq." The buttons referred to Iraqi sisters in their religious order and to the people they served there, both Muslims and Christians.

Do you have family in Iraq? How about Mexico? Vietnam?

Jesus says you do, if you follow him.

In today's Gospel Jesus' relatives come to pull him away from the crowd. But Jesus won't leave. Instead he uses the moment to teach. He tells the crowd that his family is larger than his blood relatives, or even his ethnic group or nation. Jesus' family—and your family, if you follow him—includes all people who do God's will. Notice that he includes *all* people who do God's will, not just his disciples. That means our family includes non-Christians as well.

This was a radical statement to make in Jesus' time, when family and tribal connections were so important. And it's still pretty radical during our time, when many people find it hard to care about people who are different or who live in faraway countries.

So . . . immigrants working here illegally to help their families back home? Our family. Muslims in Iraq? Our family. Jews in Israel? Our family. Homeless folks who walk our streets? Our family. The lonely kid who seems to have no friends at school? Our family.

This could change things—couldn't it?

Take :10 Reflect

If a word or phrase from the Gospel grabs your heart, sit quietly for several minutes and repeat it to yourself, asking God to show you how it applies to your life. Or, reflect and possibly journal on the following question:

* Think of the people in our world, community, or school whom you see as most different from you. If you saw them as family, how would it change your ideas or treatment of them?

Let It Take You Over

Take :05 Examine

How did I live out last week's Gospel message? What was tough? What was rewarding?

Take :05 Read

Jesus said to the crowds: "This is how it is with the kingdom of God; it is as if a man were to scatter seed on the land and would sleep and rise night and day and through it all the seed would sprout and grow, he knows not how. Of its own accord the land yields fruit, first the blade, then the ear, then the full grain in the ear. And when the grain is ripe, he wields the sickle at once, for the harvest has come."

He said, "To what shall we compare the kingdom of God, or what parable can we use for it? It is like a mustard seed that, when it is sown in the ground, is the smallest of all the seeds on the earth. But once it is sown, it springs up and becomes the largest of plants and puts forth large branches, so that the birds of the sky can dwell in its shade." With many such parables he spoke the word to them as they were able to understand it. Without parables he did not speak to them, but to his own disciples he explained everything in private.

Jesus was a big threat to the people with power—all because he told simple stories like the one in this Gospel.

The mustard seed is a small seed that spreads quickly and stubbornly. It can take over an entire garden. According to Jesus, God's Kingdom can grow in the same way. It can spread quickly through all areas and relationships in our lives. Quickly and stubbornly, Jesus says, God can inspire his disciples to spread through society working for the poor, the powerless, and the outcasts. That's bad news for the people whose power and profit is based on keeping others poor and powerless.

So it's not that hard to see why powerful men wanted him dead.

Jesus' message is still explosive and threatening to people who abuse power and profits today. That's why Christians are being martyred throughout the world. That's why Christian teens in the United States sometimes feel like outcasts.

Does God's Kingdom invade all areas of your life—school, sports, family, work, friends, weekends, wallet? Do you let Jesus' values of compassion, respect, forgiveness, and sacrifice for the powerless take root in all those areas? The more God's Kingdom spreads, the more you might face resistance from some people, especially those who say Jesus' words are unrealistic or idealistic. They might even call you a Jesus freak. But the more you get to know Jesus, the more you won't feel right unless you let it spread. Why? Because you'll see how your life more and more provides "shade" for so many people who need you.

Take :10 Reflect

If a word or phrase from the Gospel grabs your heart, sit quietly for several minutes and repeat it to yourself, asking God to show you how it applies to your life. Or, reflect and possibly journal on the following question:

- In what area of your life is it hardest to let God reign?

He Still Calms Storms

Take :05 Examine

How did I live out last week's Gospel message? What was tough? What was rewarding?

Take :05 Read

On that day, as evening drew on, Jesus said to his disciples: "Let us cross to the other side." Leaving the crowd, they took Jesus with them in the boat just as he was. And other boats were with him. A violent squall came up and waves were breaking over the boat, so that it was already filling up. Jesus was in the stern, asleep on a cushion. They woke him and said to him, "Teacher, do you not care that we are perishing?" He woke up, rebuked the wind, and said to the sea, "Quiet! Be still!" The wind ceased and there was great calm. Then he asked them, "Why are you terrified? Do you not yet have faith?" They were filled with great awe and said to one another, "Who then is this whom even wind and sea obey?"

When I was a teen, people told me I was living the "best years of my life." I'd like to find the guy who first came up with that. I'm not sure he was ever a teen.

Sure, the teen years can bring tons of fun. But they also bring plenty of storms. One day may bring new friends and great times, while the next day might bring broken friendships and loneliness. You might have successes. But you might also feel more and more pressure to succeed. Some people are pretty popular, but feel confused on the inside. Meanwhile, other people struggle to find one friend to accept them as they are.

Yep, for all the good times, there are plenty of times when we feel like the Apostles in this week's Gospel, cringing in the boat during a storm, calling out to Jesus, "Don't you care?"

Many of the early Christians felt that way. Mark wrote his Gospel for a community of Christians who were facing persecution. This story reminded those early Christians that Jesus *does* care, even though it seemed at times like he had forgotten them.

Jesus calms storms today in many ways. He might send people to us when we reach out for help. He might fill our heart with peace when we pour out our troubles in prayer or go to Mass. He might send us to calm the storms others face as they go through tough times or face persecution for taking Christian stands.

But Jesus *does* calm storms today. Call out to him, and your clouds will part.

Take :10 Reflect

If a word or phrase from the Gospel grabs your heart, sit quietly for several minutes and repeat it to yourself, asking God to show you how it applies to your life. Or, reflect and possibly journal on the following question:

- What storms need calming in your life or in the lives of people you know?

Thirteenth Sunday of Ordinary Time
Mark 5:21–43 or Mark 5:21–24; 35b–43

Don't *Have* Faith, *Act* with Faith

Take :05 Examine

How did I live out last week's Gospel message? What was tough? What was rewarding?

Take :05 Read

There was a woman afflicted with hemorrhages for twelve years. She had suffered greatly at the hands of many doctors and had spent all that she had. Yet she was not helped but only grew worse. She had heard about Jesus and came up behind him in the crowd and touched his cloak. She said, "If I but touch his clothes, I shall be cured." Immediately her flow of blood dried up. She felt in her body that she was healed of her affliction. Jesus, aware at once that power had gone out from him, turned around in the crowd and asked, "Who has touched my clothes?" But his disciples said to Jesus, "You see how the crowd is pressing upon you, and yet you ask, 'Who touched me?'" And he looked around to see who had done it. The woman, realizing what had happened to her, approached in fear and trembling. She fell down before Jesus and told him the whole truth. He said to her, "Daughter, your faith has saved you. Go in peace and be cured of your affliction." (Mark 25–34)

I know a woman just like the woman in this week's Gospel.

Teresa moved from Mexico to the United States without her family. That was hard, but it allowed her to work three jobs and save money to move the whole family here. Through all the hard and lonely times, she had faith that Jesus would help her realize her dream.

The entire family now has been living here for many years, and things are going well—all because of Teresa's faith.

Real faith means taking the initiative and showing courage. Real faith means risking rejection and failure. The bleeding woman was unclean under Jewish law, which means she risked a humiliating rejection by wading through the crowd to touch Jesus. Teresa faced loneliness, poverty, and racism. But both women showed real faith by pushing on anyway.

Do you need healing or help? Do you want to see changes in your school, your family, or your world? Do you see others that need help? Then don't *have* faith, *act* with faith. Take the risky steps to reach out and make a difference. Call for Jesus to strengthen your courage. Don't give up when it gets tough. Eventually you will feel his power flow through your life.

Take :10 Reflect

If a word or phrase from the Gospel grabs your heart, sit quietly for several minutes and repeat it to yourself, asking God to show you how it applies to your life. Or, reflect and possibly journal on the following questions:

• Who inspires you by how they take initiative and show courage for their faith? When have you shown initiative or courage in acting on your faith?

Take a Fresh Look

Take :05 Examine

How did I live out last week's Gospel message? What was tough? What was rewarding?

Take :05 Read

Jesus departed from there and came to his native place, accompanied by his disciples. When the sabbath came he began to teach in the synagogue, and many who heard him were astonished. They said, "Where did this man get all this? What kind of wisdom has been given him? What mighty deeds are wrought by his hands! Is he not the carpenter, the son of Mary, and the brother of James and Joses and Judas and Simon? And are not his sisters here with us?" And they took offense at him. Jesus said to them, "A prophet is not without honor except in his native place and among his own kin and in his own house." So he was not able to perform any mighty deed there, apart from curing a few sick people by laying his hands on them. He was amazed at their lack of faith.

Sometimes we know people so well that we miss God calling out to us through them.

"That's just my mom; she's *supposed* to say that."

"I don't care what John says; I know *all about* him!"

Friends and family. They make stupid mistakes. They sometimes say one thing and do another. They're very ordinary—sometimes even irritating. Is it hard to believe that God might be working through them to teach or help you?

In the Bible, prophets were people God chose to challenge, advise, or comfort ordinary people and rulers. Many people in Nazareth couldn't imagine that God had chosen this guy Jesus, this guy they watched grow into a local carpenter. They thought they knew all about him already. So their minds were closed when he began his ministry. Sadly, the Gospel tells us that their closed minds limited Jesus' power to help them.

Do our closed minds about some people limit God's power to improve our lives?

It can be hard to remember that God uses ordinary, everyday folks in our lives to do extraordinary things for us. Parents aren't perfect. But watch and listen closely this week for evidence that God is teaching you through them. This week, look closely at family members, or at friends you've known for years. When you drop your expectations or prejudices about them, you might see God challenging or helping you in ways you'd never expect. And don't be discouraged when a friend, coworker, or teammate writes off your advice or ignores your help; that doesn't mean God isn't *trying* to use you.

God still chooses prophets, but many are rejected by those who know them best.

Take :10 Reflect

If a word or phrase from the Gospel grabs your heart, sit quietly for several minutes and repeat it to yourself, asking God to show you how it applies to your life. Or, reflect and possibly journal on the following question:

- When was I last surprised by an insight or action by someone about whom I thought I knew everything?

What You Need Versus What Gets in the Way

Take :05 Examine

How did I live out last week's Gospel message? What was tough? What was rewarding?

Take :05 Read

Jesus summoned the Twelve and began to send them out two by two and gave them authority over unclean spirits. He instructed them to take nothing for the journey but a walking stick—no food, no sack, no money in their belts. They were, however, to wear sandals but not a second tunic. He said to them, "Wherever you enter a house, stay there until you leave. Whatever place does not welcome you or listen to you, leave there and shake the dust off your feet in testimony against them." So they went off and preached repentance. The Twelve drove out many demons, and they anointed with oil many who were sick and cured them.

Pauline and Ryan know the difference.

Both were Church leaders as teens. As young adults they decided to follow Jesus, like the disciples in this week's Gospel. Since then each has traveled around the world on trips to serve and pray with people. They often talk about how rich their lives have been. Both have even decided to become full-time ministers.

Both also live rich lives without a lot of stuff. And both have kept close Christian friends with whom they share their hopes and struggles. You see, they know the difference between what they need to follow Jesus and what gets in the way.

Let's go back to the Gospel. Jesus gives his disciples awesome power. Go drive out demons, he says. But he also tells them how to do it. Take few possessions with you and stick together.

Look now at our culture. Commercials preach that life is meaningless without the newest "stuff." Oftentimes friendships, family, and service suffer because stuff, or working long hours to afford stuff, becomes more important.

It can't be that way with Jesus' disciples. Jesus gave us all power to drive out demons. Today's demons include poverty, prejudice, loneliness, and violence. We can't do it alone. We need one another to follow Jesus long-term, because it's darn tough and full of disappointments. Possessions aren't bad, but they must not divert us from fighting today's demons or from forming the friendships that support us.

So this week remember that Jesus has given you power the world needs. The next time you feel like buying something, pray about whether the money or time you plan to spend could be more helpful to a friendship or to people who have much less. Then keep your eyes open for people who are waiting for you to set them free. Like Pauline and Ryan, you'll find yourself in places you've never dreamt of visiting.

Take :10 Reflect

If a word or phrase from the Gospel grabs your heart, sit quietly for several minutes and repeat it to yourself, asking God to show you how it applies to your life. Or, reflect and possibly journal on the following question:

- How have possessions or the pressure to get them made it harder for you to live Jesus' mission?

And Jesus Said, "Chill Out!"

Take :05 Examine

How did I live out last week's Gospel message? What was tough? What was rewarding?

Take :05 Read

The apostles gathered together with Jesus and reported all they had done and taught. He said to them, "Come away by your-selves to a deserted place and rest a while." People were coming and going in great numbers, and they had no opportunity even to eat. So they went off in the boat by themselves to a deserted place. People saw them leaving and many came to know about it. They hastened there on foot from all the towns and arrived at the place before them.

When he disembarked and saw the vast crowd, his heart was moved with pity for them, for they were like sheep without a shepherd; and he began to teach them many things.

For several years the brothers and priests of my religious order invited our neighbors to join us monthly for an hour of quiet meditation and chant in our small chapel. The congregation usually included fifteen to fifty teens from our school.

Over refreshments after the prayer, teens would often tell me how much the meditation helped relieve the stress caused by school, sports, friends, and family. So I was happy they escaped for an hour with us.

And that's what Jesus wants for his disciples in this week's Gospel. They've just come back from doing his work.

They could keep working; there were plenty of people who needed help. But Jesus says, "Come away . . . and rest."

In other words, take time to chill out. Authentic discipleship requires downtime for prayer, laughs, naps, and talk about life.

Our society seems to get busier and busier. Teens and adults seem to have more responsibilities and less time to relax. But life gets more complicated, more painful, less rewarding, and less Christian when it gets too busy.

Overworked people pray less, which means they lose God's guidance. Overworked people lose their patience more quickly, which makes it easy to snap at friends or family and difficult to forgive. Overworked people think less thoroughly and listen less often, which makes it easy to make bad decisions.

So make sure you get away. Life is about building relationships, not completing tasks. Given the pressure in our society to stay busy, you might even have to schedule downtime. Then take it. God wants it for you.

Take time with friends. Laugh. Hang out. Take naps. Build in ten-minute "rest stops" with God, when you just close your eyes and imagine Jesus wrapping his arms around you. You'll find life more rewarding and Christian living more doable.

In other words, just chill out.

Take :10 Reflect

If a word or phrase from the Gospel grabs your heart, sit quietly for several minutes and repeat it to yourself, asking God to show you how it applies to your life. Or, reflect and possibly journal on the following question:

- Is your life too hectic? Identify one thing you could do to build in more downtime.

You've Got the Bread!

How did I live out last week's Gospel message? What was tough? What was rewarding?

When Jesus raised his eyes and saw that a large crowd was coming to him, he said to Philip, "Where can we buy enough food for them to eat?" He said this to test him, because he himself knew what he was going to do. Philip answered him, "Two hundred days' wages worth of food would not be enough for each of them to have a little." One of his disciples, Andrew, the brother of Simon Peter, said to him, "There is a boy here who has five barley loaves and two fish; but what good are these for so many?" Jesus said, "Have the people recline." Now there was a great deal of grass in that place. So the men reclined, about five thousand in number. Then Jesus took the loaves, gave thanks, and distributed them to those who were reclining, and also as much of the fish as they wanted. When they had had their fill, he said to his disciples, "Gather the fragments left over, so that nothing will be wasted." So they collected them, and filled twelve wicker baskets with fragments from the five barley loaves that had been more than they could eat. (John 6:5–13)

Matt was pretty nervous, but I knew he had it in him.

He was a high school teen going with me to another high school to give a speech about a program to help homeless families. Our high school had joined the program. Matt had a passion for helping homeless people that I knew would inspire the other school's teachers and parents to join the program too.

He reminded me of the boy in this week's Gospel. Jesus and his disciples are with a huge crowd. Jesus wants to feed them, but his disciples are a bit clueless about how to do it. Then a boy comes forward, possibly inspired by the Lord's teaching, and offers his own food.

You know the rest. Jesus takes the boy's offering, multiplies the loaves, and everyone eats.

Too often adults treat teens as if they're too young to have good ideas. And, unfortunately, too often teens don't trust their own ideas or lack the self-confidence to voice them. As a result, I think we lose good teen ideas for living the Gospel and changing the world.

Our Church needs your "bread," your wisdom. Our Church ministries are poorer without teen ideas and enthusiasm. Our world comes closer to God's Kingdom each time a teen speaks up and says, "I think we should . . ." So speak up. Don't back down if people treat you like you are too young. Sure, listen to everyone, avoid stubbornness, and let other people help shape your ideas. But the Spirit is aching to speak through you.

Remember Matt? Jesus is still using young people's gifts to feed the poor.

Take :10 Reflect

If a word or phrase from the Gospel grabs your heart, sit quietly for several minutes and repeat it to yourself, asking God to show you how it applies to your life. Or, reflect and possibly journal on the following question:

- When have you backed down from sharing your opinion because you thought you were too young?

Bread of Life 1: Food for the Struggle

Take :05 Examine

How did I live out last week's Gospel message? What was tough? What was rewarding?

Take :05 Read

Jesus answered them and said, . . . "Do not work for food that perishes but for the food that endures for eternal life, which the Son of Man will give you. For on him the Father, God, has set his seal." So they said to him, "What can we do to accomplish the works of God?" Jesus answered and said to them, "This is the work of God, that you believe in the one he sent." So they said to him, "What sign can you do, that we may see and believe in you? What can you do? Our ancestors ate manna in the desert, as it is written: He gave them bread from heaven to eat." So Jesus said to them, "Amen, amen, I say to you, it was not Moses who gave the bread from heaven; my Father gives you the true bread from heaven. For the bread of God is that which comes down from heaven and gives life to the world."

So they said to him, "Sir, give us this bread always." Jesus said to them, "I am the bread of life; whoever comes to me will never hunger, and whoever believes in me will never thirst." (John 6:26–35)

I've stopped closing my eyes to pray after I receive Communion. Now I pray by watching everyone else come forward for the body and blood.

And, boy, does it move me.

Every shape and size. Every skin color. Young and old. Male and female. They come forward because they know something is missing. I know some are thinking about today's ballgame. But others are thinking about a dying relative. Each, I believe, even those people who are zoning out, is there because down deep they hunger for something the world will never offer.

"I am the bread of life," Jesus tells the crowd this week. Come to me and never be hungry.

Many people in our world work hard to convince us that we are hungry for everything—possessions, wealth, power, sex, alcohol, beauty—everything but Jesus. But down deep, aren't we really hungry for love we can count on and a chance to impact the world?

Jesus is that love. Jesus offers that chance. And Mass is where we take all he offers us and *physically* make his promises, hope, and life part of us.

I stopped going to Mass for many years. Now I see what I've missed. It's a time for healing when I hurt. It's a time to remember who loves me when I'm lonely. It's a time to renew my confidence when I doubt that I can make a difference.

Mass offers food for life's struggles—real food that satisfies—as opposed to "junk food," like power, wealth, sex, and alcohol, that always leaves you hungry. This week at Mass, remember your deepest hungers. Watch as hunger brings so many others forward during Communion. Be nourished.

Take :10 Reflect

If a word or phrase from the Gospel grabs your heart, sit quietly for several minutes and repeat it to yourself, asking God to show you how it applies to your life. Or, reflect and possibly journal on the following question:

- What could you do to make Mass more meaningful or more relevant to your life?

Bread of Life 2: Food to Share

Take :05 Examine

How did I live out last week's Gospel message? What was tough? What was rewarding?

Take :05 Read

The Jews murmured about Jesus because he said, "I am the bread that came down from heaven," and they said, "Is this not Jesus, the son of Joseph? Do we not know his father and mother? Then how can he say, 'I have come down from heaven'?" Jesus answered and said to them, "Stop murmuring among yourselves. No one can come to me unless the Father who sent me draw him, and I will raise him on the last day. It is written in the prophets: They shall all be taught by God. Everyone who listens to my Father and learns from him comes to me. Not that anyone has seen the Father except the one who is from God; he has seen the Father. Amen, amen, I say to you, whoever believes has eternal life. I am the bread of life. Your ancestors ate the manna in the desert, but they died; this is the bread that comes down from heaven so that one may eat it and not die. I am the living bread that came down from heaven; whoever eats this bread will live forever; and the bread that I will give is my flesh for the life of the world."

(Note: It might help to review last week's reflection before reading this one.)

I know some teens who think the Mass never ends—that it just continues outside the Church as they live the Gospel.

Imagine if the Communion procession would keep moving right out the door after Communion to feed our world that is starving for peace, companionship, and forgiveness.

Jesus makes it clear in this week's Gospel. He gives his bread for "the life of the world." This means that each Sunday's Gospel, homily, prayers, and Communion aren't really for us. Mass is for the world. Mass feeds us, feeds our deepest hungers, so that we can take strength, hope, and peace into the world.

Sometimes Catholics don't see the connection between Sunday and the other six days of the week. But it's there. Classmates need our acceptance. Family members need our forgiveness. Opponents in sports need our sportsmanship. People at work need our honesty. Poor and sick people need our compassion.

The more we give all that, the more we'll need Mass to recharge. The more we go to Mass, the more convinced we will be to give all that.

I remember a service retreat where a group of teens spent a week with me at a soup kitchen. One day a couple of us talked about how our daily service there made us "hungrier" for our time at Mass.

Not hungry for Mass? Try living the Gospel even more radically this week, and see what that does.

Take :10 Reflect

If a word or phrase from the Gospel grabs your heart, sit quietly for several minutes and repeat it to yourself, asking God to show you how it applies to your life. Or, reflect and possibly journal on the following question:

- How might your understanding of Communion change if you envision yourself sharing part of your host with people you see each day of the week?

Twentieth Sunday of Ordinary Time
John 6:51–58

Bread of Life 3: Food That Changes You

Take :05 Examine

How did I live out last week's Gospel message? What was tough? What was rewarding?

Take :05 Read

Jesus said to the crowds:"I am the living bread that came down from heaven; whoever eats this bread will live forever; and the bread that I will give is my flesh for the life of the world."

The Jews quarreled among themselves, saying,"How can this man give us his flesh to eat?" Jesus said to them,"Amen, amen, I say to you, unless you eat the flesh of the Son of Man and drink his blood, you do not have life within you. Whoever eats my flesh and drinks my blood has eternal life, and I will raise him on the last day. For my flesh is true food, and my blood is true drink. Whoever eats my flesh and drinks my blood remains in me and I in him. Just as the living Father sent me and I have life because of the Father, so also the one who feeds on me will have life because of me. This is the bread that came down from heaven. Unlike your ancestors who ate and still died, whoever eats this bread will live forever."

The early Christians scared some Romans. It came from scary rumors that Christians "ate flesh and drank blood."

It should be scary—because you can't keep going to Communion regularly without being challenged to change. And change can be scary.

John wrote this week's Gospel to show early Christians the importance of the Eucharist. He wanted to show that

God loves us so much, he wants to physically connect with us. By reflecting on the Gospel and sharing Christ's body and blood at the Eucharist, we develop a real physical intimacy with God. The person who takes Communion "remains in me and I in him," Jesus says. That's the gift. But that's also the scary part—because Jesus can change us.

Intimacy, real friendship, changes us. Intimate friends become part of us. We take on some of their interests. We hang out in some of their spots. We start to see the world through their eyes. Friendship also shows itself physically through handshakes, hugs—even friendly punches.

All this happens through Mass. The Gospels ask us to take on God's interests (forgiveness and peace) and to hang out where Jesus hung out (with the forgotten). We physically connect with the Lord in Communion, but also during the sign of peace and our greetings to friends and neighbors. The more we go to Mass with open eyes and ears, the more our own eyes and ears will change the rest of the week. Our eyes will see the work God needs done, and our ears will hear the cries that break his heart.

Are you ready for that?

Take :10 Reflect

If a word or phrase from the Gospel grabs your heart, sit quietly for several minutes and repeat it to yourself, asking God to show you how it applies to your life. Or, reflect and possibly journal on the following question:

• How have you started to see things differently or hear more cries for help as you've grown closer to God?

He Knows Rejection

Take :05 Examine

How did I live out last week's Gospel message? What was tough? What was rewarding?

Take :05 Read

Many of Jesus' disciples who were listening said, "This saying is hard; who can accept it?" Since Jesus knew that his disciples were murmuring about this, he said to them, "Does this shock you? What if you were to see the Son of Man ascending to where he was before? It is the spirit that gives life, while the flesh is of no avail. The words I have spoken to you are spirit and life. But there are some of you who do not believe." Jesus knew from the beginning the ones who would not believe and the one who would betray him. And he said, "For this reason I have told you that no one can come to me unless it is granted him by my Father."

As a result of this, many of his disciples returned to their former way of life and no longer accompanied him. Jesus then said to the Twelve, "Do you also want to leave?" Simon Peter answered him, "Master, to whom shall we go? You have the words of eternal life. We have come to believe and are convinced that you are the Holy One of God."

It must've hurt when they started to walk away from him.

Jesus had wowed the crowds with his healing powers and charismatic teaching. But then they heard the tough news. Maybe the sacrifice sounded too great. Maybe he was asking too much.

Regardless, they all started to walk away. Finally, Jesus looked at his closest friends and said, "Do you also want to leave?" We know the answer. They said they'd hang around. But they eventually fled too, after the Last Supper.

It can be lonely following Jesus and trying to follow his example in every part of life. It means saying no to a lot of things that many people see no problem doing—abusing alcohol or drugs, gossiping, having sex before marriage, being dishonest, cheating—and yes to a lot of things people want no part of—helping poor people, standing against violence, choosing forgiveness over vengeance. It can cause conflicts with friends, coworkers, and family who don't believe as strongly as you do.

But "to whom shall we go?" Jesus does have the answer to eternal life—life to the fullest now and through eternity. Jesus is the answer to the problems facing our broken world. He also knows the pain of rejection. You're likely to face it too if you keep following him.

Just remember, true friends won't reject you for making Christian choices. Those who do so aren't true friends. And also remember, Jesus knows the pain. So when you hurt from rejection, spend time with him in prayer and let him offer comfort and strength.

Take :10 Reflect

If a word or phrase from the Gospel grabs your heart, sit quietly for several minutes and repeat it to yourself, asking God to show you how it applies to your life. Or, reflect and possibly journal on the following question:

• When have you faced rejection because of a Christian choice?

Just Sticks and Stones?

Take :05 Examine

How did I live out last week's Gospel message? What was tough? What was rewarding?

Take :05 Read

When the Pharisees with some scribes who had come from Jerusalem gathered around Jesus, they observed that some of his disciples ate their meals with unclean, that is, unwashed, hands.——For the Pharisees and, in fact, all Jews, do not eat without carefully washing their hands, keeping the tradition of the elders. And on coming from the marketplace they do not eat without purifying themselves. And there are many other things that they have traditionally observed, the purification of cups and jugs and kettles and beds.——So the Pharisees and scribes questioned him, "Why do your disciples not follow the tradition of the elders but instead eat a meal with unclean hands?" He responded, "Well did Isaiah prophesy about you hypocrites, as it is written:

This people honors me with their lips,
    but their hearts are far from me;
in vain do they worship me,
    teaching as doctrines human precepts.

You disregard God's commandment but cling to human tradition." He summoned the crowd again and said to them, "Hear me, all of you, and understand. Nothing that enters one from outside can defile that person; but the things that come out from within are what defile.

"From within people, from their hearts, come evil thoughts, unchastity, theft, murder, adultery, greed, malice, deceit, licentiousness, envy, blasphemy, arrogance, folly. All these evils come from within and they defile."

"Sticks and stones will break my bones, but words will never hurt me." Right.

I have a problem. My mouth runs light years ahead of my brain. That means I too often say things and hurt others without thinking.

Jesus is right. What comes out of us can make us impure. Our words build up or tear down. First, our words of ridicule can destroy others. Some people feel put down all the time. Your words of praise might make their day.

Second, our words shape how we think about people. Do we focus only on faults when we talk about some people? If so, we are likely to miss the good within those people. Doesn't God focus mostly on the good things about us?

Third, our words also shape how others think about people. We can take the opportunity to point out people's strengths when others tear them down. We also can take the opportunity to stop gossip when it comes across our path. Isn't that what we want others to do for us?

Jesus calls the Pharisees hypocrites in this week's Gospel. That word comes from a Greek word meaning "actors." This week, as you talk to and about other people, make sure your words show that your Christianity is not just an act.

Take :10 Reflect

If a word or phrase from the Gospel grabs your heart, sit quietly for several minutes and repeat it to yourself, asking God to show you how it applies to your life. Or, reflect and possibly journal on the following question:

- Who inspires you by his or her refusal to gossip or say unkind words about others?

Be Opened!

Take :05 Examine

How did I live out last week's Gospel message? What was tough? What was rewarding?

Take :05 Read

Again Jesus left the district of Tyre and went by way of Sidon to the Sea of Galilee, into the district of the Decapolis. And people brought to him a deaf man who had a speech impediment and begged him to lay his hand on him. He took him off by himself away from the crowd. He put his finger into the man's ears and, spitting, touched his tongue; then he looked up to heaven and groaned, and said to him, "Ephphatha!"—that is, "Be opened!"—And immediately the man's ears were opened, his speech impediment was removed, and he spoke plainly. He ordered them not to tell anyone. But the more he ordered them not to, the more they proclaimed it. They were exceedingly astonished and they said, "He has done all things well. He makes the deaf hear and the mute speak."

Sometimes I stop rushing around and realize that I rarely hear birds singing.

I stay pretty busy. My mind stays pretty focused on the next task or appointment. And I miss the birds. And I fear I miss other cries as well—the cries of people who need me.

"Be opened!" Jesus commands in this week's Gospel. He restores a man's hearing and gives him the power to speak. I wonder what the man heard after that. I bet he heard the sighs of lonely people who needed his time. I bet he stopped and sat with them. I bet he heard pleas of hunger from poor people. I bet he stopped and fed them. I bet he heard the cries of people who were rejected or suffering. I bet he stopped and embraced them.

Many people in our families, our schools, our jobs, and our world need our ears opened. Many don't want our advice. They just want us to listen without judgment while they talk about what hurts. Others need us to stand up with and for them at school or in our community. They need us to listen closely to understand their problems. Others, like parents and mentors, are trying to offer us advice for life. They need us to listen to their wisdom without getting defensive.

Do we hear their cries or advice as we go through life? Or do we rush so quickly that we miss them? This week, each day, ask Jesus to open your ears so you can listen closely. People will come across your path who need you to listen, or to whom you need to listen.

Take :10 Reflect

If a word or phrase from the Gospel grabs your heart, sit quietly for several minutes and repeat it to yourself, asking God to show you how it applies to your life. Or, reflect and possibly journal on the following question:

- What can keep me from really listening to people who need my help or who are offering me advice?

The Hard Truth

Take :05 Examine

How did I live out last week's Gospel message? What was tough? What was rewarding?

Take :05 Read

Jesus and his disciples set out for the villages of Caesarea Philippi. Along the way he asked his disciples, "Who do people say that I am?" They said in reply, "John the Baptist, others Elijah, still others one of the prophets." And he asked them, "But who do you say that I am?" Peter said to him in reply, "You are the Christ." Then he warned them not to tell anyone about him.

He began to teach them that the Son of Man must suffer greatly and be rejected by the elders, the chief priests, and the scribes, and be killed, and rise after three days. He spoke this openly. Then Peter took him aside and began to rebuke him. At this he turned around and, looking at his disciples, rebuked Peter and said, "Get behind me, Satan. You are thinking not as God does, but as human beings do."

He summoned the crowd with his disciples and said to them, "Whoever wishes to come after me must deny himself, take up his cross, and follow me. For whoever wishes to save his life will lose it, but whoever loses his life for my sake and that of the gospel will save it."

There is no Christianity without a cross. And if we want to follow, we have to take up the cross. That's the hard truth.

Taking up the cross doesn't mean coping well with sickness or bad luck. We take up the cross when we choose sacrifice we could avoid in order to help others.

Here's a brief story.

Mark was a volunteer when our school helped house homeless families for a week. We needed volunteers to come Sunday
morning to help serve breakfast. Mark came early, even though
Saturday night had been the prom. Mark was the only student to
show up. He was tired. But he chose to sacrifice. And homeless
families had a better day because of it.

Living as a Christian means choosing little sacrifices like Mark's
on a daily basis. Taking up the cross means giving up your life each
day in little ways. You take up your cross when you help your
Mom without her asking you. You take up your cross when you
reach out to the unpopular kid. You take up your cross when you
sacrifice time at the mall for time at the soup kitchen.

Like Peter, each day we must decide who we think Jesus is. We
show that he is our Messiah (the one who came to save us) when
we choose to sacrifice for others. Oddly enough, it is through
those little sacrifices that we really save our own lives—and add
to the lives of others.

Take :10 Reflect

If a word or phrase from the Gospel grabs your heart, sit quietly
for several minutes and repeat it to yourself, asking God to show
you how it applies to your life. Or, reflect and possibly journal on
the following question:

- When have you chosen a sacrifice—taken up a cross—that has
  shown others who Jesus is to you?

You Don't Compare?

Take :05 Examine

How did I live out last week's Gospel message? What was tough? What was rewarding?

Take :05 Read

Jesus and his disciples left from there and began a journey through Galilee, but he did not wish anyone to know about it. He was teaching his disciples and telling them, "The Son of Man is to be handed over to men and they will kill him, and three days after his death the Son of Man will rise." But they did not understand the saying, and they were afraid to question him.

They came to Capernaum and, once inside the house, he began to ask them, "What were you arguing about on the way?" But they remained silent. They had been discussing among themselves on the way who was the greatest. Then he sat down, called the Twelve, and said to them, "If anyone wishes to be first, he shall be the last of all and the servant of all." Taking a child, he placed it in the their midst, and putting his arms around it, he said to them, "Whoever receives one child such as this in my name, receives me; and whoever receives me, receives not me but the One who sent me."

Competition and comparison—our culture thrives on them.

Television has made a killing on it in recent years. Who will win the job as apprentice to the millionaire? Who will win as the top model? Who will get voted off the island?

Competition can spur us on, but it also can tear us up inside. Why can't I look like her? Why can't I shoot the ball like him? I know teens that tear themselves down because they constantly focus on how they don't measure up to others. We need to stop comparing ourselves with others and start loving ourselves for who we are—like God loves us.

In this week's Gospel, Jesus' disciples are competing to be the best. Stop comparing yourself to others, Jesus tells them. Look inside yourself, get to know your special talents and use them for the least in our society. Jesus pulled a child aside because children were valued least in that society, some Scripture scholars say.

According to Jesus your value doesn't come from appearance or popularity or how well you compete. It comes from God. And if you really want to feel great, go out into the world and show the people who are not valued just how valuable they are. Is your talent making kids laugh? Develop it. Are you good at listening and offering comfort? Do that more often. Maybe you like building things. Give your time to help build a house for a poor family.

So relax. You've got nothing to prove. Turn off the reality shows and turn on the Gospel. You'll feel a lot prouder when you look in the mirror.

Take :10 Reflect

If a word or phrase from the Gospel grabs your heart, sit quietly for several minutes and repeat it to yourself, asking God to show you how it applies to your life. Or, reflect and possibly journal on the following question:

- What talent or gift do I have or can I develop to help people who need me?

The Good Type of Pain

How did I live out last week's Gospel message? What was tough? What was rewarding?

[Jesus said,] "Whoever causes one of these little ones who believe in me to sin, it would be better for him if a great millstone were put around his neck and he were thrown into the sea. If your hand causes you to sin, cut it off. It is better for you to enter into life maimed than with two hands to go into Gehenna, into the unquenchable fire. And if your foot causes you to sin, cut it off. It is better for you to enter into life crippled than with two feet to be thrown into Gehenna. And if your eye causes you to sin, pluck it out. Better for you to enter into the kingdom of God with one eye than with two eyes to be thrown into Gehenna, where 'their worm does not die, and the fire is not quenched.'" (Mark 42–43,45,47–48)

I know a young man who gave up smoking pot. It was hard because it was part of his daily routine. He smoked when he was sad. He smoked to celebrate. He smoked to fight boredom. In some ways pot became part of him. So when he gave it up, it felt like cutting off part of his body. But after breaking free, he realized how much more alive he felt and how much stronger his friendships became.

Jesus knows what he's talking about in this week's Gospel.

Sure, his advice sounds pretty extreme. But his point is right on. Sin can become routine. A sinful habit can become so normal, so much a part of us, that we can't imagine life without it and can't see how it hurts us or others.

That goes for any sinful habit: sex outside of marriage, alcohol or drug abuse, selfishness, dishonesty, prejudice. The list can go on.

The lesson from this week's Gospel is this: We have to break some habits, even though that can hurt, because they keep us from the life God promised us. Our lives can be wasted if we aren't willing to make tough choices and let go of some things we think we need that conflict with the Gospel.

Where do you start? Look at how you live daily. How do you party, date, study, treat family and friends, spend money? When you take a hard look, do you see any habits that conflict with the Gospel? If you're not sure, ask a friend, parent, or Catholic minister who will be honest with you. If you find a sinful habit, then ask for God's strength to "cut it off." It will be hard at first. But you'll be thankful in the long run.

Take :10 Reflect

If a word or phrase from the Gospel grabs your heart, sit quietly for several minutes and repeat it to yourself, asking God to show you how it applies to your life. Or, reflect and possibly journal on the following question:

- What habits that are or could be sinful have you broken or do you need to break?

How Are You Relating?

Take :05 Examine

How did I live out last week's Gospel message? What was tough? What was rewarding?

Take :05 Read

The Pharisees approached Jesus and asked, "Is it lawful for a husband to divorce his wife?" They were testing him. He said to them in reply, "What did Moses command you?" They replied, "Moses permitted a husband to write a bill of divorce and dismiss her." But Jesus told them, "Because of the hardness of your hearts he wrote you this commandment. But from the beginning of creation, God made them male and female. For this reason a man shall leave his father and mother and be joined to his wife, and the two shall become one flesh. So they are no longer two but one flesh. Therefore what God has joined together, no human being must separate." In the house the disciples again questioned Jesus about this. He said to them, "Whoever divorces his wife and marries another commits adultery against her; and if she divorces her husband and marries another, she commits adultery." (Mark 10:2–12)

My parents divorced. And for a while I wondered what God thought about that—especially because of this passage.

But Jesus isn't condemning divorced people here. He's raising important questions about relationships. First, do we give up too easily on them? We live in a culture that doesn't like pain. Too often people break off relationships instead of working through problems that come up. It hurts to forgive. It's humbling to say, "I'm sorry." But we never learn how to love and be loved unless we work on relationships—even when it hurts.

Second, are we willing to give of ourselves in our relationships? We live in a culture that breeds selfishness. Too often people break off relationships because they don't get *what they want* from them. But relationships are two-way streets. And the strongest and happiest ones feature two people willing to sacrifice for each other.

Finally, do we support or weaken relationships? As Jesus says, people shouldn't interfere with healthy relationships, because God is their source. It's our job to help people build their relationships and keep them healthy. So don't let jealousy spark you to interfere with friends who are dating. Watch out for misplaced loyalty that urges you to help a friend be dishonest with parents, a boyfriend, or a girlfriend. Celebrate your parents' anniversary with them. If your mom or dad is single, offer support if he or she starts dating.

Don't take this passage simplistically. Sometimes, even though we would wish otherwise, there are parents who cannot live together any longer. Instead, let this passage challenge how you commit to relationships and how you support those you love in their relationships.

Take :10 Reflect

If a word or phrase from the Gospel grabs your heart, sit quietly for several minutes and repeat it to yourself, asking God to show you how it applies to your life. Or, reflect and possibly journal on one of the following questions:

- Where do you struggle in building relationships? How have you supported others' relationships?

Drop Your Bags!

Take :05 Examine

How did I live out last week's Gospel message? What was tough? What was rewarding?

Take :05 Read

As Jesus was setting out on a journey, a man ran up, knelt down before him, and asked him, "Good teacher, what must I do to inherit eternal life?" Jesus answered him, "Why do you call me good? No one is good but God alone. You know the commandments: You shall not kill; you shall not commit adultery; you shall not steal; you shall not bear false witness; you shall not defraud; honor your father and your mother." He replied and said to him, "Teacher, all of these I have observed from my youth." Jesus, looking at him, loved him and said to him, "You are lacking in one thing. Go, sell what you have, and give to the poor and you will have treasure in heaven; then come, follow me." At that statement his face fell, and he went away sad, for he had many possessions.

Jesus looked around and said to his disciples, "How hard it is for those who have wealth to enter the kingdom of God!"
(Mark 10:17–23)

How would Jesus finish this sentence if he looked at you and said: "Follow me. You'll have treasure in heaven if you go and . . ."

The man in this week's Gospel wanted to follow. Maybe Jesus had grabbed his heart or given him hope that things could be much better. But something held him back—

wealth. Jesus knew that possessions held the man hostage, and he offered him freedom. But the man couldn't accept it.

We all carry "baggage," something that's slowing us down, keeping us from following Jesus more closely. That's partly because our society breeds attachment to such baggage. For some of us, possessions hold us back. Jesus spends some extra time talking about possessions because he knows that people with a lot of possessions can easily become possessed by them.

Here are a couple of other examples. Our society also breeds attachment to revenge. Don't get mad; get even. But revenge breeds revenge. And people who can't forgive are held hostage by the anger that sears their hearts.

Our society breeds attachment to pride as well. Don't show your weakness. Never let them see you sweat. But people who never show weakness are phony, and people who never apologize end up lonely.

Jesus wants to help us let go. He offers us strength through prayer and Mass, guidance through the Scriptures and other Christians, forgiveness when we reattach to our baggage by sinning.

So look honestly at your baggage. What's keeping you from a life of love and service? But don't go away sad. Over time our Savior will help you drop it all.

Take :10 Reflect

If a word or phrase from the Gospel grabs your heart, sit quietly for several minutes and repeat it to yourself, asking God to show you how it applies to your life. Or, reflect and possibly journal on the following question:

- What might Jesus tell you to drop if you asked him how you could follow him more closely?

Pay the Ransom

Take :05 Examine

How did I live out last week's Gospel message? What was tough? What was rewarding?

Take :05 Read

James and John, the sons of Zebedee, came to Jesus and said to him, "Teacher, we want you to do for us whatever we ask of you." He replied, "What do you wish me to do for you?" They answered him, "Grant that in your glory we may sit one at your right and the other at your left." . . .

When the ten heard this, they became indignant at James and John. Jesus summoned them and said to them, "You know that those who are recognized as rulers over the Gentiles lord it over them, and their great ones make their authority over them felt. But it shall not be so among you. Rather, whoever wishes to be great among you will be your servant; whoever wishes to be first among you will be the slave of all. For the Son of Man did not come to be served but to serve and to give his life as a ransom for many." (Mark 10:35–37, 41–45)

A few years ago, teen hazing rituals were making news.

Reports told how teen leaders humiliated and sometimes physically injured younger teens as a way to initiate them into sports teams or school traditions. One ritual called for football players to hold down, strip, and humiliate younger players. Another encouraged school leaders to throw garbage on younger students. Some "just" called for older teens to surround and intimidate younger teens in school hallways.

Hazing has always saddened and angered me. It frightens or hurts young teens. It teaches teens to enjoy humiliating others. It holds up failed leadership as good leadership.

I think failed leadership saddened and angered Jesus too. In this Gospel Jesus sees how James and John are looking for leadership perks that will give them power over others. Was he angry or sad when he told all the Apostles, "It shall not be so among you"? Who knows? But Jesus saw how leaders in his time abused authority and used it to abuse others, especially those who were weak. He was determined to teach his leaders to use authority differently. He used his life as the model to follow.

Jesus' life was a ransom, he says. That means it freed people. And, like Jesus, teen leaders have the ability to free younger teens or to imprison them. Hazing imprisons teens in fear and humiliation. But teen leaders can free younger teens by befriending them, by defending them, by helping them learn new skills, and by showing them how to sacrifice for others.

Jesus clearly defines Christian leadership, and asks you to consider whether you will offer it to teammates, classmates, and younger brothers and sisters. Will your life be a ransom for others?

Take :10 Reflect

If a word or phrase from the Gospel grabs your heart, sit quietly for several minutes and repeat it to yourself, asking God to show you how it applies to your life. Or, reflect and possibly journal on the following question:

- In what ways could you be a ransom, that is, an offer of freedom, for people who are held hostage to fear, loneliness, or despair?

Do You Want to See?

Take :05 Examine

How did I live out last week's Gospel message? What was tough? What was rewarding?

Take :05 Read

As Jesus was leaving Jericho with his disciples and a sizable crowd, Bartimaeus, a blind man, the son of Timaeus, sat by the roadside begging. On hearing that it was Jesus of Nazareth, he began to cry out and say, "Jesus, son of David, have pity on me." And many rebuked him, telling him to be silent. But he kept calling out all the more, "Son of David, have pity on me." Jesus stopped and said, "Call him." So they called the blind man, saying to him, "Take courage; get up, Jesus is calling you." He threw aside his cloak, sprang up, and came to Jesus. Jesus said to him in reply, "What do you want me to do for you?" The blind man replied to him, "Master, I want to see." Jesus told him, "Go your way; your faith has saved you." Immediately he received his sight and followed him on the way.

Some days I just don't want to see anymore.

The nightly news shows people starving across the world. I see homeless people on my street corner. That lonely person who never seems to fit in comes to me needing some extra time when I'm already busy and tired. Honestly, I don't want to see at times because I get tired of trying to help. I want to focus on just my life, my wants, my friends, my pleasure.

Have you been there?

If so, you're a pretty normal Christian. If so, Bartimaeus is a good person to think about. He called out to Jesus, asking for sight. Jesus granted his request. And when Bartimaeus could see, he stood up and followed Jesus.

Bartimaeus reminds us that we have a choice. We can be blind. We can turn away from people and problems that call us to show compassion and sacrifice. Or we can ask Jesus to help us see.

But Christians sometimes focus their vision just on helping others. The good thing is that Jesus helps us see more than that—a lot more. He helps us see how valuable we are to God and how much God loves us regardless of our strengths or weaknesses. He helps us see the good friends coming into our lives through our service and discipleship. He helps us see that we can't help everyone—that it's critical to say no at times in order to rest, relax, and avoid burning out from helping others.

So don't feel down when you want to just turn away. Ask Jesus to help you see why you should turn back to him and where you can find the support you need to keep going. He'll show you. He always shows me. And, like Bartimaeus, you'll "see" that the best choice in life is to get up and start following Jesus again.

Take :10 Reflect

If a word or phrase from the Gospel grabs your heart, sit quietly for several minutes and repeat it to yourself, asking God to show you how it applies to your life. Or, reflect and possibly journal on the following question:

• What are the hardest things for me about life as a Christian?

Body and Soul: Train Them for God

Take :05 Examine

How did I live out last week's Gospel message? What was tough? What was rewarding?

Take :05 Read

One of the scribes came to Jesus and asked him, "Which is the first of all the commandments?" Jesus replied, "The first is this: Hear, O Israel! The Lord our God is Lord alone! You shall love the Lord your God with all your heart, with all your soul, with all your mind, and with all your strength. *The second is this:* You shall love your neighbor as yourself. There is no other commandment greater than these." *The scribe said to him, "Well said, teacher. You are right in saying, 'He is One and there is no other than he.' And 'to love him with all your heart, with all your understanding, with all your strength, and to love your neighbor as yourself' is worth more than all burnt offerings and sacrifices." And when Jesus saw that he answered with understanding, he said to him, "You are not far from the kingdom of God." And no one dared to ask him any more questions.*

Our school's swimmers once asked to use the chapel before state competition. Their goal was to spend time meditating, to let God calm them so they could swim their best.

Our bodies, souls, minds, and hearts are connected. You can't devote one toward a goal successfully without devoting all the others as well. Judaism has always taught that. Drawing on his Jewish faith, Jesus emphasizes loving God with your whole self: your heart, your understanding, and your strength.

Like sports, discipleship requires training your entire self, which takes time. But you never develop the skills unless you start practicing. So here are some tips if you're ready for training.

Body. Get enough sleep. It's hard to show compassion when you're tired. Discipline your appetites. Excessive food and drink creates health problems that can keep you from serving others. Sex outside of marriage cheapens both people and risks creating an unwanted child.

Mind. Think about your faith. Challenge it. Debate it with committed Christians. Pay close attention in religion class. Learn why millions let it guide their lives. Read the newspaper. Think about the answers our faith offers for today's problems.

Soul. Pray daily. Listen— don't just talk—in prayer. Take five-minute breaks with God during the day. Let God remind you that Jesus is with you regardless of what happens.

Heart. Let yourself feel for people who suffer—the kid who never fits in, the hungry person at a soup kitchen, or the sick person dying of AIDS. Don't lock up your emotions when you hurt. Express them to people you trust to help you sort them out.

Remember that it takes time to develop any skill. So be patient with yourself as you train for discipleship. God's not concerned with how well you do. The Lord just wants to see you practicing

Take :10 Reflect

If a word or phrase from the Gospel grabs your heart, sit quietly for several minutes and repeat it to yourself, asking God to show you how it applies to your life. Or, reflect and possibly journal on the following question:

- On which part of my whole self do I need to spend more time in training for discipleship: my body, my mind, my soul, or my heart?

Keep an Eye Out for Widows

Take :05 Examine

How did I live out last week's Gospel message? What was
tough? What was rewarding?

Take :05 Read

*In the course of his teaching Jesus said to the crowds, "Beware of
the scribes, who like to go around in long robes and accept
greetings in the marketplaces, seats of honor in synagogues, and
places of honor at banquets. They devour the houses of widows
and, as a pretext, recite lengthy prayers. They will receive a very
severe condemnation."*

*He sat down opposite the treasury and observed how the
crowd put money into the treasury. Many rich people put in
large sums. A poor widow also came and put in two small coins
worth a few cents. Calling his disciples to himself, he said to
them, "Amen, I say to you, this poor widow put in more than all
the other contributors to the treasury. For they have all contributed from their surplus wealth, but she, from her poverty, has
contributed all she had, her whole livelihood."*

I remember a youth-group president I met in a Central
American village. He proudly told me how his group
collected food for poor people in his community each
Christmas. I later saw the youth-group president's home—
a thatched hut he shared with a large family. Despite his
poverty he focused on helping other people.

That youth-group president has become one of my role
models. I hope that I can someday show generosity like
that.

Jesus talks about role models in this week's Gospel. He contrasts the scribes and the rich people with the widow. The scribes, Jesus says, draw attention to themselves, seeking the crowd's praise. Some rich people make large donations, but none that require real sacrifice. Meanwhile, a widow quietly sacrifices from her meager income to offer something to her religion. Widows were some of the poorest people in ancient Israel.

Where do you look for role models? Our culture often promotes modern-day scribes as role models for teens to follow—athletes and corporate CEOs who flaunt their wealth, politicians who love their power, and religious leaders who profit from their connections to powerful people.

Jesus says, look for another way if you are seeking a life of holiness. Search out people who make quiet but significant sacrifices for others. Think about your parents. How have they sacrificed to improve your life? How about your teachers? Many teachers don't make a lot of money, but stay committed to teaching because they like helping young people. Don't forget the people who are working at your parish. Church workers often work long hours for low pay because they believe the world needs to hear Jesus' message.

Adolescence is the time to look around for people who can be models for your life. If you want to take Jesus up on his offer of a full life, keep an eye out for the modern-day "widows."

Take :10 Reflect

If a word or phrase from the Gospel grabs your heart, sit quietly for several minutes and repeat it to yourself, asking God to show you how it applies to your life. Or, reflect and possibly journal on the following question:

- Who reminds you of the widow in the Gospel passage?

When the World Is Falling Apart

Take :05 Examine

How did I live out last week's Gospel message? What was tough? What was rewarding?

Take :05 Read

Jesus said to his disciples:
"In those days after that tribulation the sun will be darkened,
and the moon will not give its light,
and the stars will be falling from the sky,
and the powers in the heavens will be shaken.
"And then they will see 'the Son of Man coming in the clouds'
with great power and glory, and then he will send out the angels
and gather his elect from the four winds, from the end of the
earth to the end of the sky.
"Learn a lesson from the fig tree. When its branch becomes
tender and sprouts leaves, you know that summer is near. In the
same way, when you see these things happening, know that he is
near, at the gates. Amen, I say to you, this generation will not
pass away until all these things have taken place. Heaven and
earth will pass away, but my words will not pass away.
"But of that day or hour, no one knows, neither the angels in
heaven, nor the Son, but only the Father."

We've all had those days. The sun is shining, but everything seems so dark. It's a peaceful night, but pain fills our heart. It seems like the world is ending.

Breaking up with a girlfriend or boyfriend, fighting with a parent, feeling rejected by a friend, failing a test—any or all of these can bring our world crashing down. Things can get even worse for practicing Christians, who face even more difficulties at times because of the tough stands we must take to do the right thing.

This week's Gospel was written to give you courage during the tough times. The early Christians faced rejection and persecution. Mark's Gospel reminded them that Jesus is with his followers during the toughest of times. Even though everything may seem to be falling apart, Jesus' words "will not pass away."

That means that despite the troubles you face, you can rest assured God loves you, God is reaching out to comfort you, and God will strengthen you. Yes, God is with you when you are alone. But often God wants you to reach out to others. As humans, we often need other humans to really feel God's embrace. Friends, counselors, family, or members of your Church often bring Christ's help during tough times. So don't isolate yourself when you hurt, or you might be keeping God's help at a distance.

Don't give up and turn away, because in the midst of your toughest times, you can see God's "power and glory."

Take :10 Reflect

If a word or phrase from the Gospel grabs your heart, sit quietly for several minutes and repeat it to yourself, asking God to show you how it applies to your life. Or, reflect and possibly journal on the following question:

- When have you found God helping you out when part of your world seemed to be falling apart?

Patriotic Catholic or Catholic Patriot?

Take :05 Examine

How did I live out last week's Gospel message? What was tough? What was rewarding?

Take :05 Read

Pilate said to Jesus, "Are you the King of the Jews?" Jesus answered, "Do you say this on your own or have others told you about me?" Pilate answered, "I am not a Jew, am I? Your own nation and the chief priests handed you over to me. What have you done?" Jesus answered, "My kingdom does not belong to this world. If my kingdom did belong to this world, my attendants would be fighting to keep me from being handed over to the Jews. But as it is, my kingdom is not here." So Pilate said to him, "Then you are a king?" Jesus answered, "You say I am a king. For this I was born and for this I came into the world, to testify to the truth. Everyone who belongs to the truth listens to my voice."

Dorothy Day was a twentieth-century Catholic hero. During the Great Depression, she founded the Catholic Worker movement to help poor people and to challenge the nation to adopt laws that reflected Catholic values. She opposed war as a solution to world problems. She also fought for laws that protected workers. She went to jail several times for nonviolently protesting U.S. policies that she thought violated the Gospel.

Dorothy loved her nation. But Jesus was her king. Like him, she "testified to the truth" even when it put her in conflict with her country and a majority of its citizens. We're called to be like her.

Jesus tells Pilate in this week's Gospel that he has no earthly kingdom. Jesus wasn't a politician, but he hoped to reshape society—government and religion—to reflect God's Kingdom. That's the work we carry on as his followers. For disciples the cross always rises above the flag. We're called to be Catholic patriots, people whose faith shapes our patriotism; not patriotic Catholics, people who place national policies above Gospel values. Patriotism for Christians means using our political system to shape a more compassionate, peaceful nation—being a seed of Jesus' Kingdom. That might cause conflict with other Americans at times. And it might cause us—like Dorothy Day—to protest when the politicians seem to be deaf.

Our nation separates church and state. That means the state can't tell you what religion to follow. It doesn't mean that Christian values should be separated from our political life. Christ calls us as disciples to trace each of our political opinions back to the Gospel. How does the Gospel challenge our national policies on poverty? on health care? on war and peace? on criminal justice? on abortion?

Here's the question to ask when we make decisions about whether to support a politician's proposal: If Jesus was our king, would he enact this?

Take :10 Reflect

If a word or phrase from the Gospel grabs your heart, sit quietly for several minutes and repeat it to yourself, asking God to show you how it applies to your life. Or, reflect and possibly journal on the following questions:

- What government policy would you want to see changed because of your faith in Christ the King? What can you do to help change it?